Anne Brontë's Radical Vision:
Structures of Consciousness

ELIZABETH HOLLIS BERRY

Anne Brontë's Radical Vision: Structures of Consciousness

English Literary Studies
University of Victoria
1994

ENGLISH LITERARY STUDIES
Published at the University of Victoria

Founding Editor
Samuel L. Macey

GENERAL EDITOR
Robert M. Schuler

EDITORIAL BOARD
Thomas R. Cleary
Evelyn M. Cobley
Kathryn Kerby-Fulton
Victor A. Neufeldt
Stephen A. C. Scobie

ADVISORY EDITORS
David Fowler, *University of Washington*
Donald Greene, *University of Southern California*
Juliet McMaster, *University of Alberta*
Richard J. Schoeck, *University of Colorado*
Arthur Sherbo, *Michigan State University*

BUSINESS MANAGER
Hedy Miller

ISBN 0-920604-74-9

The ELS Monograph Series is published in consultation with members of the Department by ENGLISH LITERARY STUDIES, Department of English, University of Victoria, P.O. Box 3070, Victoria, B.C., Canada, v8w 3w1.

ELS Monograph Series No. 62
© 1994 by Elizabeth Hollis Berry

Cover: Charlotte Brontë's watercolor portrait of Anne Brontë is reproduced by courtesy of The Brontë Society, Brontë Parsonage Museum, Haworth, West Yorkshire.

To my mother, L. M. B., and in memory of my father, S. F. B.

CONTENTS

Preface   11

Chapter 1
  Poetical and Critical Beginnings:
  "Where knotted grass neglected lies"   13

Chapter 2
  Agnes Grey:
  "Pillars of Witness" in "The Vale of Life"   39

Chapter 3
  The Tenant of Wildfell Hall:
  From Hearth's "Desperate Calmness"
  To Heath's "Loftiest Eminence"   71

Conclusion
  "Her outward seeming and her inward mind"   108

Notes   111

Bibliography   118

ACKNOWLEDGMENTS

The idea of studying Anne Brontë was first suggested by Juliet McMaster who kept a watchful eye on the first version of the project as my supervisor. Sara Stambaugh read the manuscript and supported the idea of publication.

Kind words of encouragement and scholarly sustenance also came from Patricia Demers. The final manuscript could not have been written without the generous help of Michael Rawdon, whose own kind of radical vision (and computer expertise) sustains and challenges the post-graduate pilgrim along the way.

Anne Brontë was fortunate enough to have a beloved Aunt Elizabeth who watched over her work and so was I. My thanks go to Bess, Maud Harriet, and Nin, the three sisters who introduced me variously to creative endeavor, long walks, sea cliffs, poetry, women's writing, and Anne Brontë's eloquent world of primroses and bluebells.

Thanks also to Diana for driving me up to Haworth one sunny day to look at the parsonage and the letters. I particularly want to thank those who kept the home fires burning (and sometimes supper), offering imaginative suggestions about Anne Brontë's relationship with Charlotte, her love of seawater, her ability to command all my attention and the sibling rivalry in the Brontë family. Thank you Victoria, Thomas, Laura, and Sân.

PREFACE

The purpose of this study is to examine Anne Brontë's poetry and prose fiction, with particular reference to prevalent image patterns in her work. Bearing in mind that she has been critically undervalued, I wish initially to consider why this may have occurred and then to establish the scope of poetical language that shapes her texts. Viewed as a body of valuable work from a young writer, her writings merit close reading for their combination of realistic societal analysis with the poetical embodiment of feeling.

In each chapter, the examination of imagery focuses on Brontë's antithetical method which explores social structures and their inherent dichotomies. Her analyses of contemporary society represent such problems as inequality, isolation, alcoholism, and abuse through an interlocking system of images which connect external setting with internal reality. Throughout Brontë's writings, these recurrent images of structural elements have a dual function in that they both describe aspects of the physical environment—households, landscapes, seasons—and provide an evocative poetical structure that underpins her texts. Brontë's strategy is to use linked images of enclosed and open spaces to realize emotional states and to trace the psychological and spiritual development of character.

Initially in her poems and later in her prose fiction, Anne Brontë places the philosophical or social dialectic in a supporting framework of material settings, ranging from smouldering hearth to windswept heath, each of which sets an emotional tone for her inquiry into life's meanings. Such iterative natural and spatial images provide a figurative commentary on experience that links the outer world's natural or social structures with the inner consciousness of both her poetic persona and her fictional characters. Referring to psycho-social structures (through contrasting images of high and low places, harsh and soft spaces), even as it adds poetic or narrative structure to the text, this stylistically and psychologically constructive imagery—which I shall thus call "structural imagery"—creates subtle definitions and redefinitions within Brontë's texts.

Although the stated purpose of her novels is didactic, the imagery in both her poetry and prose fiction exploits the complexities of language as an instrument for depicting and re-defining the human condition. Establishing the strength of her contribution to the novel in particular, a closer study of Anne Brontë's writings reveals the radical vigor and penetrating authenticity of her work.

CHAPTER 1

Poetical and Critical Beginnings: "Where knotted grass neglected lies"

Variously consoling, poignant, or arresting in their imagery and purpose, Anne Brontë's poems frequently embody the beginnings of her fiction. Referring to her own physical background in the moors' beloved landscape of "knotted grass," where "weeds usurp the ground," the poet recalls "my home" from her distant position at Thorp Green, longing for the familiar forms of "my barren hills" and "wilderness of heath."[1] In this poem "Home," Anne Brontë's evocative natural images combine with structural elements to invoke the source of her artistic and spiritual vision in the reassuringly solid but broadly open dimensions of her childhood's wild moorland spaces, encompassed by the gray drystone walls that define the landscape:

> Restore me to that little spot,
>   With gray walls compassed round
> Where knotted grass neglected lies,
>   And weeds usurp the ground.   (100)

When she yearns to be restored to the place (and thus restored or recreated in herself), Anne Brontë's verse recalls the defining shapes of home which comfort and inspire her. The contrast between the second stanza's "softly smiling skies" and the preferred "barren hills" or "wilderness of heath" suggests a radical vision which insists on replacing conventional expectations of softly smiling ease or complacency with pictures of harsher ground.

Although the later "Self-Communion" is an important record of Anne Brontë's inner struggles, this earlier poem is significant for its emphasis on the landscape of home as a key to her developing consciousness, providing an analogy between setting and emotion which is a recurrent motif in her writings. The powerful longing for a less cultivated milieu of weeds and knotted grass communicates the poet's own singular identity, staunchly setting her apart from society's comfortable places and asserting her independence. Repeatedly throughout her poetical writings, verses like "Home" tackle issues which emerge more fully in the narratives of *Agnes Grey* and *The Tenant of Wildfell Hall*: the struggle to understand and cope with life's pain, the attempt to reconcile spirit with material experience, the effort to find meaning in the familiar knots of her background, and the determination to define an independent self.

Often expressing a more personal voice, poems such as "Self-Communion" lend themselves to an autobiographical reading which pinpoints the intensely private inner struggles for autonomy which Anne Brontë goes on to characterize openly in her fiction:

> I saw that they were sundered now,
> The trees that at the root were one:
> They yet might mingle leaf and bough,
> But still the stems must stand alone.   (157)

This memorable vision of a "sundered" tree is central to the implied biographical import of "Self-Communion." Through suggestive layers of meaning, the image of forceful but natural separation works dramatically to assert Anne Brontë's own identity as something separate from that of her two sisters, particularly Emily whose spirit was often twinned with hers. Although their creative activity "might mingle leaf and bough," she points out emphatically that "the stems must stand alone."[2] This symbolic tree is doubly useful. In addition to providing an example of Anne Brontë's effective use of nature imagery to define character development, it also makes a plea for the first step in establishing a critical reappraisal of her work: she must be allowed to stand alone, distinct from her more famous sisters.

If one accepts Edward Chitham's claim that "Self-Communion" is a crucial record of Anne Brontë's development, then it is curious that his final comment still maintains the sense of conditional approval which has so often been reserved for the youngest of the Brontë sisters: he refers to her as "one who might have been able to contribute material of high value if she had lived."[3] The implication that she had not yet written material of outstandingly high value may be true of her poetry (with some notable exceptions), but her fiction is another matter.

The early death of any writer leads to speculation about great works of art that might have been, and, in Anne Brontë's case, there are not only those sorts of reductive, speculative comments to contend with, but also unfavorable comparisons with the "bright twin stars" of her sisters. Against their brilliance, one short-sighted reviewer in 1897 saw Anne Brontë swimming into view as a "third mild-shining star of the tenth magnitude, which otherwise would have remained invisible."[4] Certainly,

Anne Brontë's death at the age of twenty-nine, leaving a modest literary legacy of only two novels and fifty-nine lyric poems, must prompt tantalizing questions about unrealized potential. Despite critics' statements to the contrary, however, her artistic skill and vision were far from unproven. Her achievement, albeit small in quantity, is manifestly substantial in quality. For posterity, Anne Brontë has left solid proof of an accomplished, questioning, radical eye in an impressive body of work that includes her poems and her two novels, *Agnes Grey* and *The Tenant of Wildfell Hall.*

Initially, however, Anne Brontë was not even given her due as far as the authorship of these two novels was concerned. From the outset, confusion was rife about which of the "Bell" brothers—Currer, Ellis, or Acton—wrote which novels. This confusion about the pseudonymous brothers Bell was worsened significantly by the efforts of Emily's and Anne's unscrupulous publisher, Thomas Newby. Newby, whom Charlotte later dubbed "needy as well as tricky,"[5] boldly attempted to capitalize on the success of Charlotte's *Jane Eyre* by offering the American rights of *The Tenant* to a New York firm, claiming that it was yet another work by the same Currer Bell who had, according to Newby, written both *Wuthering Heights* and *Agnes Grey*, but who had evidently changed his name as the work progressed.

The controversy about the Bells caused more than a ripple in the literary world, particularly in North America, where, in an intriguing twist, Anne Brontë's powerful talent was discerned in all three sisters' works, her unknown (supposedly male) identity allowing her the critical freedom to be attributed a forceful writing style that she was denied by later critics who knew of her identity as the "gentle, retiring, inexperienced writer" characterized by Charlotte.[6] One E. P. Whipple, writing for the *North American Review* in 1848, exemplifies the confusion about the Bell "firm." He refers to Acton Bell as "the author of *Wuthering Heights, The Tenant of Wildfell Hall,* and, if we mistake not, of certain offensive but powerful portions of *Jane Eyre.*" He goes on to discuss Acton's forensic literary abilities: "Acton, when left together to his imaginations, seems to take a morose satisfaction in developing a full and complete science of human brutality."[7] One cannot avoid the suspicion that Anne Brontë's literary reputation would have been altogether improved if she had remained cloaked in the guise of the brutal Acton and had never emerged as the gentle Anne.

When Newby had originally published *Agnes Grey*, its comparative brevity (at least by Victorian standards) allowed him to append it as a third volume to the two volumes of *Wuthering Heights*. The novels were inevitably compared—to the detriment of Anne Brontë's entirely unrelated (one might say purposively antithetical) text. The anonymous reviewer in *The Atlas* (1848) felt that *Agnes Grey* lacks "the power and originality of *Wuthering Heights*" and that it "leaves no painful impression on the mind—some may think it leaves no impression at all."[8] In the same year, the unsigned notice by George Henry Lewes in the *Westminster Review* judged *Jane Eyre* to be "decidedly the best novel of the season,"[9] and the tendency to perceive Acton as the least powerful of the Bell brothers thus became established. To the present day, this view of Anne Brontë as a diminution of her brilliant sisters remains the standard by which to measure her work. As Elizabeth Langland points out in *Anne Bronte: The Other One*, despite positive contemporary reviews of *The Tenant of Wildfell Hall* in the *Athenaeum* and *Literary World*, critics throughout the century followed Mrs. Gaskell's description of Anne as less "original" than Emily, and even feminist critics[10] have tended to rediscover Charlotte to the exclusion of Anne, having, in Langland's words, "surprisingly little to say about Anne Brontë."[11]

Some insight into the differing roles adopted by (and ascribed to) the sisters may emerge from one of Anne Brontë's few surviving letters. In a letter to Charlotte's friend Ellen Nussey, Anne Brontë pictures herself as someone who is "deficient" in her "organ of language," and about to be "engulphed in a letter of Charlotte's."[12] This amusingly ironic remark sums up what ultimately happened to obscure her talent: she was somehow "engulphed" by her sisters' literary reputation. This was not, however, because her "organ of language" was in any way deficient: indeed, Anne Brontë's language was manifestly proficient, but of a different order.

Whether one need look any further than this same dominant sister Charlotte to find what Derek Stanford calls the "evil fairy" in the story of Anne Brontë's literary reputation is a moot point.[13] Charlotte Brontë's own comments provide evidence that she did indeed initiate a lukewarm response to her younger sister's work. Writing to W. S. Williams in 1847 and 1848, she uses such phrases as "simple pathos" and "quiet description" to describe the novel *Agnes Grey*, whereas Emily Brontë's work merits the much stronger epithets "vigorous" and "original."[14] That Charlotte may well have used her sister's governess story as a starting point for *Jane Eyre* explains some of her carefully measured judgment on the matter. Discriminating between the novels in a similarly judicious vein, perhaps even protective of her sister's reputation, after Anne

Brontë's death it was Charlotte who vetoed the re-issuing of *The Tenant* because, as she wrote again to W. S. Williams at Smith, Elder & Co., "*Wildfell Hall* it hardly appears to me desirable to preserve."[15] Whatever the reasons, this decision of Charlotte Brontë's resulted in a kind of literary banishment for the effectively silenced younger sister.

Adopting what became the commonly-held, dismissive approach, T. W. Reid wrote in 1877 (in his monograph on Charlotte) that neither of Anne Brontë's novels "will really repay perusal."[16] In the marketplace of literary economy, he suggests, Anne Brontë is worthless currency; such a statement as this would then guarantee her literary product a dearth of interest, especially in the context of Victorian obsessions with the idea of material reward for effort. As George Moore later pointed out, Anne Brontë thus became the "Cinderella" of the Brontë sisters.[17] Again, the colorful metaphor drawn from fairy tales suggests her banishment as if by magic, whereas the cause lies manifestly in the more pragmatic area of critical neglect. By "leaving Anne in the kitchen," as Moore puts it, what the critics missed was the possibility that her novels might actually "repay perusal" tenfold if treated to a less partial, more balanced reading. Anne Brontë's novels demand that the reader determinedly put aside critical preconceptions of "weakness" or "lack of color"[18] in order to focus on the obvious strengths of her radical vision, embodied in the probing analyses and powerful narratives of her fiction. The radical nature of her vision can be seen in a penetrating story-telling technique which builds a recognizable world of images, both describing an existing order and seeking to redefine it.

Both *Agnes Grey* and *The Tenant* contain compelling analyses of contemporary society and suggest possible responses to the problems of inequality, infidelity, isolation and abuse. My view is that the subtle re-definitions within Anne Brontë's texts are advanced by her use of structural imagery, which, with its reference to contrasting seasons and settings, its metaphorical embodiment of social displacement or spiritual reconciliation, and its implied comparisons of inner and outer worlds, builds thematic patterns, giving her narratives an organic unity and radical strength. Prefiguring the detailed psycho-social polemic of her narratives, Anne Brontë's poems repeatedly examine philosophical cruxes, problems of personal identity or spiritual and social consciousness, which she later explicates at length in her novels through the astute characterization of diverse figures. One can trace a progression of ideas and strategies from the often simple lyric of her verse to the complex interweavings of embedded narratives (tales wrapped within tales) in her last novel *The*

Tenant; the larger worlds of her prose fiction thus issue from her poems which explore similar ground in miniature, by means of a more personal voice.

From the Gondal poetry through to the last verses written just prior to her death in 1849, Anne Brontë's poems reflect the underlying struggles expressed by her fictional characters for spiritual understanding in a materially disparate, emotionally troubling world. Image patterns in the poems show a questing spirit endeavoring to form (and reform) psychological or social structures, creating secure areas of comforting hope in the "restless toil and vanity" or "dreadful darkness" of a life in which she sees her poetic self striving as a "pilgrim through this vale of tears" (Chitham 123, 163, 152). One recognizes this poetic persona as a recurrent figure whose search for spiritual liberation gives rise to similar pilgrimages through the vale of life undertaken by certain key fictional characters in the novels.

A recurring image in the Gondal poems, as in all Anne Brontë's writings, is the enclosed space of a dark prison. In "The Captive's Dream," for example, the character of Alexandrina Zenobia laments her imprisonment:

> I struggled wildly but it was in vain,
> I could not rise from my dark dungeon floor,
> And the dear name I vainly strove to speak,
> Died in a voiceless whisper on my tongue . . .   (62)

These images also symbolize what Anne Brontë described in the letter to Ellen Nussey as the supposed deficiency in her "organ of language." The physical imprisonment parallels an emotional imprisonment here, a connection which occurs frequently in Anne Brontë's writing, and this is also linked with a physical inability to verbalize emotion—the voice is stopped when the character strives to speak. This image of voicelessness is later dealt with at some length in *Agnes Grey*, where silence and volubility are contrasted to provide social commentary.

In "A Voice from the Dungeon," written in 1837 when Anne Brontë was seventeen and away from home at Roe Head school, her Gondal character Marina Sabia also dreams of liberty as she dwells immured in isolation:

> This place of solitude and gloom
> Must be my dungeon and my tomb.   (60)

Although these images of tomb-like solitude can be read as the Byronic preoccupations of a young writer who knew but later eschewed the Romantic vision, only three years later, in August 1840 when Anne Brontë was again away from home working as a governess to the Robinson family, herself feeling isolated from her loved ones, "Lines Written at Thorp Green" uses similar imagery of lonely, isolated longing. While evidently autobiographical, the later poem expresses a comparable sense of emotional desolation in a poignantly simple lyric. The first stanza recalls the stopping up of emotional expression:

> O! I am very weary
>   Though tears no longer flow;
> My eyes are tired of weeping,
>   My heart is sick of woe. (75)

The last stanza emphasizes another familiar theme in the image of "blighted" hope:

> Oh didst thou know my longings
>   For thee from day to day,
> My hopes so often blighted,
>   Thou wouidst not thus delay. (75)

Also emphasized here is the recurrent idea that direct communication of powerful longings is held in check because the speaker feels bound to keep her emotions hidden.

During the early 1840s, when Mr. Brontë's curate William Weightman (thought to be Anne's love interest) was part of the family circle at Haworth, the longing for human company leaves the poet repeatedly waiting or hoping for the presence of the beloved. Whether or not Weightman is the figure described in Anne's love poems has never been firmly established, but as Chitham points out, poems written during this period describe "a real young man"[19] who shares Weightman's characteristically sunny smile and light heart. Despite Charlotte's tendency to detract from any potential relationship between the two, we know from a letter of Charlotte's that he was a charming person who was interested in Anne. In the letter written to Ellen Nussey, Charlotte archly pictures Weightman sitting "opposite Anne at church sighing softly and looking out of the corners of his eyes to win her attention."[20] Possibly written years before its inclusion in *Agnes Grey*, "To —— —," an undated poem (placed by Chitham within this period) shows the speaker's hope sometimes thwarted by others:

> Oh, they have robbed me of the hope
> My spirit held so dear;
> They will not let me hear that voice
> My soul delights to hear.

This hope is then irrevocably dashed by death which leaves "the joys of life" and earthly love entombed forever:

> I'll weep no more thine early doom,
> But O! I still must mourn
> The pleasures buried in thy tomb
> For they will not return. (88)

These recurrent images of tomb-like spaces indicate Anne Brontë's acute awareness of life's divisions or separations, but they also attest, not surprisingly, to the pre-eminence of death in one central part of her home landscape. Not only had she suffered the deaths of loved ones, including her mother, sisters, and the beloved Weightman, but Haworth Parsonage stands literally poised atop the graveyard hill, with tombstones crowding its front wall and fields opening from its back wall, an architectural juxtaposition which must have had considerable impact on the developing consciousness of the young writer.

Mourning the loss of the loved one (most likely Weightman) again in a later poem, Anne combines images of the tomb with light imagery to convey the heart's yearning for the bright presence of the beloved "shape" (142). In an acknowledgment of death's limiting actuality, the second stanza of this untitled poem notes the humanly vulnerable shape of a sleeping body against the tomb's dark narrowness:

> I know that in the narrow tomb
> The form I loved was buried deep,
> And left, in silence and in gloom,
> To slumber out its dreamless sleep. (141)

The images of darkness and imprisonment are extended in the next stanza to include evocative details about "the corner, where it lies" and the dampness on the stones that cover the body: "The charnel moisture never dries / From the dark flagstones o'er its breast" (142). But this image of death's "slow decay" in its oppressive finality is answered in the poetic soul by the hope that through a combination of divine intervention and imaginative force, the "raptured vision" of longing will make the "pictured form" return in a "burst" of divine light:

> I, by night,
> Have prayed, within my silent room,
> That Heaven would grant a burst of light
> Its cheerless darkness to illume;
>
> And give thee to my longing eyes,
> A moment, as thou shinest now,
> Fresh from thy mansion in the skies,
> With all its glories on thy brow.
>
> Wild was the wish, intense the gaze
> I fixed upon the murky air,
> Expecting, half, a kindling blaze
> Would strike my raptured vision there,— (142)

Although the poet dismisses as "False hope!" the gleam of light which briefly transforms tomb and corpse in this dream-like vision, the bitterness of her loss is mitigated by the true hope kindled in the beloved's remembered presence:

> O, no! thy spirit lingers still
> Where'er thy sunny smile was seen:
> There's less of darkness, less of chill
> On earth, than if thou hadst not been. (143)

The poet's philosophical conclusion to this exploration of loss and longing reveals the glimmer of hope made possible only through the experience of living, of having known her loved one in life:

> Life seems more sweet that thou didst live,
> And men more true that thou wert one:
> Nothing is lost that thou didst give,
> Nothing destroyed that thou hast done. (143)

Thus ending in a tentatively hopeful tone, this poem's heartfelt expression of grief is answered in a way that often signals Anne Brontë's personal conclusions about the conflicting impulses of hope's passionate flame and experience's cold fastness.

Although these poems of lost love come from a period when Anne was maturing through grief—her hopeful young spirit altered or stifled by painful experience—several other poems explore the implied conflict between freedom and restraint of expression in an ongoing dialogue between hope and experience. This dramatized debate about the opposition between passion and rationality is expressed in certain poems that render the poet's struggle to reveal over the passage of time what Edward Chitham calls a "temptation towards hardness of heart"—a temptation

Anne Brontë recognizes in herself (38). In "Views of Life," this recognition creates a poetic persona who grapples with the conflict between reason and emotion, often sinking into the psychological prison of depression which colors every space with the shades of the tomb:

> When sinks my heart in hopeless gloom,
> When life can shew no joy for me,
> And I behold a yawning tomb
> Where bowers and palaces should be,
>
> In vain, you talk of morbid dreams,
> In vain, you gaily smiling say
> That what to me so dreary seems
> The healthy mind deems bright and gay.   (115)

Here, as in other poems and the novels, Anne Brontë conveys the imperative of emotional independence in the clear (if sobering) light of experience, "When that false light is past away" (115). Like her main fictional characters, the poetic persona expresses a rational distancing learned through the pain of isolation and disillusion, while paradoxically still maintaining the grace of connection with others through divine or familial love, seeking "A home where heart and soul may rest" (94) and clinging "To memory and hope" on the way (119).

The recognition of disturbing or destructive energy is also indicated in the poems through harsh noise linked to stormy wind imagery, a connection which is developed in the novels for the purposes of characterization, implying particular psychological traits analogous with wind or weather. Such windy representations of wild excess are associated in *Agnes Grey*, for example, with unsympathetic characters:[21] Mr. Murray, the "blustering, roystering country squire" (63), or Rector Hatfield, "sweeping along like a whirlwind" (85), both of whom exhibit the harsh "droning" tones of materialism which Anne Brontë's verse implies is a limited form of consciousness. Elizabeth Langland suggests that Anne here echoes Charlotte's characterization of St. John Rivers in *Jane Eyre*; at any rate, she expresses similar concerns with this kind of character in her poem "The Three Guides" (written in the same year as *Agnes Grey*). Since Charlotte was writing the final chapters of *Jane Eyre*, with their focus on the cold St. John Rivers—described by Charlotte as a spirit "redeemed from the earth"—at the time when "The Three Guides" was written, the connection between the Rivers character and the Spirit of Earth is a distinct possibility.[22] In "The Three Guides" Anne Brontë addresses the "Spirit of earth," whose "icy clasp" or "chill" hand holds its followers locked in the "stony-hearted grasp" of materialism (144). Its limiting hardness also evoked by ice and stone images, this spirit's "harsh, droning voice" drowns out the flight of the poet's soul on its heavenward path:

> If, to the breezes wandering near,
>   I listened eagerly,
> And deemed an angel's voice to hear
>   That whispered hope to me,
> That heavenly music would be drowned
>   In thy harsh, droning voice,
> Nor inward thought, nor sight, nor sound
>   Might my sad soul rejoice.   (145)

Significantly, the poet's search for the divine message in a cosmic harmony of sound, nature's sometimes "heavenly music," is inspired by gentle breezes which usher in the "angel's voice" of whispered hope (145).

Within her image patterns, Anne Brontë consistently sets up an opposition between the divine message—the "still, small voice of Heaven" (145)—and the excessive "output" (as Derek Stanford calls it) of the bustling materialist. Anne Brontë "criticises this view of life . . . for its want of an interior sense. It is all external action, all bustle and 'output.'"[23] Stanford's observation points to an evident division between windy materialist figures and gently spiritual characters in her writings. Such divisions (and potential bridges) are explored at length in "The Three Guides," one of the few poems to be anthologized in the nineteenth century,[24] and an important record of her philosophical belief in the synthesis of passion and reason, expressed in her writing style as a combination of poetic and didactic approaches. The "icy clasp" of this "Spirit of earth," with its "stony-hearted grasp," is reflected in an inability to hear the gentle sounds of Heaven, or to see the bridges and paths (lit by divine light) which reconcile life's hard experience with the soul's gentle faith:

> Dull is thine ear; unheard by thee
>   The still small voice of Heaven.
> Thine eyes are dim, and cannot see
>   The helps that God has given.
> There is a bridge, o'er every flood,
>   Which thou canst not perceive,
> A path, through every tangled wood;
>   But thou wilt not believe.   (145)

Turning away from this darkened, unharmonious world and choosing the Spirit of Faith to be her guide, in stanza 21 the poet describes a contrasting world of magical light and comfort:

> Meek is thine eye and soft thy voice
>   But wondrous is thy might
> To make the wretched soul rejoice,
>   To give the simple light.
> And still to all that seek thy way,
>   Such magic power is given—
> E'en while their footsteps press the clay
>   Their souls ascend to heaven. (149)

Inscribed in the closing lines of this stanza, the combined images of earth and heaven express an essential paradox in Anne Brontë's approach (both religious and literary): the transcendent impulse of the soul is activated through divine inspiration "E'en while" or, one feels, precisely *when* the feet are firmly anchored in the pragmatic "clay" of experience.

In addition to these images of empowering light, the final two stanzas (26 and 27) stress another important recurring image in Anne Brontë's work: the image of home. Responding in the penultimate stanza to the voice of love, the poet hears about "that blest home above" and finally enjoins the spirit to "bring me home at last" (150), an entreaty that intimates the longing for home expressed in so many of the poems. Throughout the poems, these central images of "home" and "light" are, as in the novels, often conflated in firelight imagery. Seen in the Gondal poem "The Consolation" (November 1843), which asserts the poet's conviction that "I know there is, though far away / A home where heart and soul may rest," the firelight image prefigures later concerns with hearth and home in both *Agnes Grey* and *The Tenant*. Simply put, the fireside in this poem offers a refuge from life's storms:

> Though bleak these woods and damp the ground
> With fallen leaves so thickly strewn,
> And cold the wind that wanders round
> With wild and melancholy moan,
>
> There *is* a friendly roof I know
> Might shield me from the wintry blast;
> There is a fire whose ruddy glow
> Will cheer me for my wanderings past. (94)

Answering the cold wind's depressing cadences with a cheerfully "ruddy glow," this fire conjoins the poet's wandering spirit with a community that offers warm acceptance.

Such images of firelight as a straightforward representation of familial comfort are not always found in Anne Brontë's writings. She sometimes uses fire imagery in an ironic way to indicate emotions such as derangement or discord, the hearth and heart interconnection acting ironically as a metaphor for unhealthy or dangerously riven social structures. A later Gondal poem of 1846 shows an imprisoned soul "in a dungeon deep," whose tormented eyes reveal "a fitful flickering fire" that figures forth both lost life and encroaching madness:

> It did not speak of reason gone,
>   It was not madness quite;
> It was a fitful flickering fire,
>   A strange uncertain light.
>
> And sooth to say, these latter years
>   Strange fancies now and then
> Had filled his cell with scenes of life
>   And forms of living men. (127)

Also seen in another poem from the same period, the characteristically alienated Gondal prisoner in his isolated Romantic setting has an unexpected parallel in the more clearly autobiographical poem, "Monday Night May 11th 1846," which is placed next to it in Chitham's conjectural chronological ordering (128). Authentically rooted in time and place, the poet's recollection of domestic discord and personal alienation describes a hearth which houses a fire, the bright red light of which is figuratively undone by the desolation of conflict among the family members:

> The fire is burning in the grate
> As redly as it used to burn,
> But still the hearth is desolate
> Till Mirth and Love with *Peace* return. (129)

Written the year before she was fully working on *The Tenant*, at a time when Anne Brontë had been revising *Agnes Grey* for publication, this fifth verse with its "desolate" hearth image reveals the same sense of emptiness felt by both Helen and Gilbert in the absence of co-equal love in *The Tenant*. Again, in the pivotal verses of "Self-Communion," which share image clusters with climactic scenes in *The Tenant*, the fire embodies the fading glow of lost love:

> Love may be full of pain, but still,
> 'Tis sad to see it so depart,—
> To watch that fire, whose genial glow
> Was formed to comfort and to cheer,
> For want of fuel, fading so,
> Sinking to embers dull and drear . . .   (156)

Initially presented in its most positive human form, the "genial glow" of the fire created for comfort poignantly evokes a chilling lack, an emotional "want of fuel," in the heart's response to losing love and shutting off a part of the self. As in *Agnes Grey* and *The Tenant*, the hearth image here functions as an emotive focus for Brontë's examination of social and spiritual divisions.

The underlying point in this poetic representation of the hearth or home without heart is that something vital is missing from the scene, a state of affairs that the poet presents through a series of positive followed by negative definitions, carving out, as it were, the hollow shape of conflict behind the familiar glow:

> The moon without as pure and calm
> Is shining as that night she shone;
> But now, to us she brings no balm,
> For something from our hearts is gone.   (128)

Asserting this manifest lack by means of a picture that implies wholeness, the moon image seems particularly apt here. The reflected light of the moon offers a kind of philosophical chiasmus which crosses image (dark planet reflecting light) with the rhetorical method employed (positive statement reflecting negative).

Similar images of light as the vehicle for "pure" heavenly comfort recur throughout the poems and in the novels. Identifying the reflected light of the moon as a previous source of healing "balm," the poet's troubled heart finds in the moon's maternal "calm" a comforting female presence which is similar to the lunar manifestation of a warning female voice (specifically a mother's voice) urging Jane to flee temptation at the climactic end of Chapter 27 in Charlotte's *Jane Eyre*. Although moon imagery is a poetic commonplace, and allusions to the ancient feminine principle represented by the moon's influence can be found in poetry throughout the centuries, its personal immediacy in Anne Brontë's poems implies (despite Aunt Elizabeth Branwell's closeness to her) how keenly felt the need for a comforting maternal figure must have been at times in the motherless Brontë household.

In "Fluctuations," an earlier poem (from 1844), the moon's female presence rises through the mist to shine "serenely" on the suffering soul, offering comforting "light and hope" with her pale beams. Contrasted with the "bright sun's most transient gleams," the moon's light, though unpromisingly "wan" and "lifeless" (suggesting a ghostly presence), provides a "blessed" release from despair. The poem's opening stanza conveys loss followed by the "serenely" comforting light of a "blessed" presence:

> What though the sun had left my sky;
>   To save me from despair
> The blessed moon arose on high
>   And shone serenely there. (103)

The salvatory connection with the poet's soul is established in the fourth stanza, where the moonlight is lost:

> But as above that mist's control
>   She rose and brighter shone
> I felt her light upon my soul,
>   But now—that light is gone! (103)

Plaintively evoking a child's lost hope in the passing of a motherly figure, the desolation caused by this passing spirit is all-encompassing:

> Thick vapours snatched her from my sight
>   And I was darkling left,
> All in the cold and gloomy night
>   Of light and hope bereft. (104)

If one reads the "thick vapours" as a metaphor for death, the poet's entreaty for the return of the moonlight in the final stanza emphasizes the power of faith in restoring the felt presence of divine comfort reflected in "that silvery gleam":

> Kind Heaven, increase that silvery gleam
>   And bid these clouds depart;
> And let her kind and holy beam
>   Restore my fainting heart. (104)

A similar representation of the moon as a "holy" figure of maternal ease and kindness appears again in "Mirth and Mourning," a later Gondal poem, as "holy moonbeams" shedding "sweet celestial balm" (132) upon those below who look heavenward for succour. This benevolent power of light is to some extent also an embodiment of Anne

Brontë's magnanimous Universalist hope for "eternal bliss" in heaven for all, regardless of Calvinist notions of the elect. She presents this hope in "A Word to the Calvinists" as a "cheering ray" of light:

> And O! there lives within my heart
> A hope long nursed by me,
> (And should its cheering ray depart
> How dark my soul would be) . . .   (89)

Such images of encouraging light, gleaming softly within the poet's consciousness, also represent the light of Faith for which she cries out to be strengthened in "A Hymn" as her soul "ascends in prayer":

> Without some glimmering in my heart,
> I could not raise this fervent prayer;
> But O a stronger light impart,
> And in thy mercy fix it there!   (91)

Light also provides a metaphor for the confident blessing of spiritual acceptance (analogous to self-acceptance) in the poem "Confidence":

> O make me wholly Thine!
> Thy love to me impart,
> And let Thy holy spirit shine
> For ever on my heart!   (114)

Seen somewhat less often in her verse, but an important indication of the heroine's progress towards independent self-discovery in the novels, this beatifically shining light suggests unequivocal joy in the commitment to a "holy" purpose, together with the experience of divine love.

Such warmly inspirational light is repeatedly figured as sunlight in the novels and in certain poems which express the feeling of being loved, an experience of rapture variously divine or human in its origin. Turning grey to gold in a way that manifestly actualizes heaven's blessings, the warm beams of sunlight which can dramatically transform the shape of the hills surrounding Haworth Parsonage re-appear in the poems and play an important part in the light imagery used throughout Anne Brontë's writings. Sunlight, according to Chitham, is for Anne Brontë the source of "warm love" (101), a connection he relates to her feelings for William Weightman, as the image of the loved one's "sunny smile" intimates. Although plausible, such a connection, suggesting the male principle traditionally represented by sun images, would limit Anne Brontë's poetic exploration of experience in a way that does not entirely fit her egalitarian, radical purpose. Images of sunlight in the poems and the novels go beyond such limited associations, referring, in "Self-Communion," for example, to an inspired place of heavenly "rest" as "that sunny shore" seen across a wide "rolling sea," in linked images that echo Agnes Grey's sunlit transformation on the seashore. Similarly, the poem "In Memory of a Happy Day in February" links sun and wind images with divine inspiration through a paradoxically negative construction (like the "desolate" fireside) which acknowledges their influence but denies their impact by affirming the force of a spiritual revelation as the underlying transformative power:

> I was alone, for those I loved
>   Were far away from me,
> The sun shone on the withered grass,
>   The wind blew fresh and free.
>
> Was it the smile of early spring
>   That made my bosom glow?
> 'Twas sweet, but neither sun nor wind
>   Could raise my spirit so. (82)

The assonance in the rhyming words emphasizes in sequence her freedom ("me"/"free"), and her ecstatic, breathless response to the liberating moment, expressed in open-mouthed but end-stopped "o" sounds ("glow"/"so"). This pattern of emphasis continues in the next two stanzas, rhyming "undefined" with "mind" and "bliss" with "this," to create a harmonious expression of transcendence, figuring forth the kind of mystical experience that passes through physical boundaries:

> Was it some feeling of delight,
>   All vague and undefined?
> No, 'twas a rapture deep and strong,
>   Expanding in my mind! (82)

In this process of soul-making, the sun and wind images offer a source of stimulus, but the actual work of re-definition occurs within, when the onlooker sees God's "wisdom and his power / In all his works displayed" (82). Significantly, the inspirational, sunlit atmosphere of the poem parallels the scene of Agnes Grey's enlightening experience on the beach, where she stands poised on the brink of a new life surrounded by a divinely endowed cosmic energy emblematized in dazzling sunlight reflected on the waters. Although such moments are far from easy to define, Anne Brontë is careful to differentiate between a vaguely felt emotion and a definitely spiritual manifestation. Not just a "vague" feeling, this impulse is deeply spiritual, originating from the divine source of rapture which is most persuasively experienced as "expanding" the mind.

Throughout Anne Brontë's writings, this idea of the mind expanding is often allied with a liberating outdoor space in the world of nature beloved, but expressed differently, by both Anne and Emily. Whereas for Emily the wild, natural world is a pantheistic embodiment of a great spirit, for Anne the realms of heaven and earth are imagined as separate spaces, with various linking bridges, portals and paths offered to the earthbound traveller who has faith and hope. Sheer unfettered delight in the freedom of the countryside is expressed in "Song," one of the later Gondal poems from September 1845:

> O happy life! To range the mountains wild,
> The waving woods—or Ocean's heaving breast,
> With limbs unfettered, conscience undefiled,
> And choosing where to wander, where to rest! (122)

But, as in the yearning here for a lost life of "the wandering Outlaw" (122), this physical freedom is usually shown in combination with longing for spiritual liberation. "Vanitas Vanitatis Etc.," which follows "Song" in Chitham's ordering of the poems, expresses the dynamic forces of nature as "endless labour everywhere" in an analogy of restless human endeavor:

> The fountains gushing from the hills,
> Supply the ever-running rills;
> The thirsty rivers drink their store,
> And bear it rolling to the shore,
> But still the ocean craves for more. (123)

The poet's conclusion that "Pleasure but doubles future pain" echoes the connection found in many of the poems between nature's powerful beauty and the personal pain of loss or longing.

In this context, although flower and plant images often figure forth the inspiring vitality of spring and the remembered joys of youth, Anne Brontë's gentle "flowerets" (usually wildflowers) are sometimes also linked with death or grief. Starting with the earliest poem, "Verses by Lady Geralda" (1836), this connection between nature and death is established when Lady Geralda remembers how, long ago, she "loved to lie / Upon the pathless moor," enjoying a series of remembered outdoor experiences that place her current situation in an even more "melancholy" light (49). Thus, despite the "pleasant scent / Of wild and lovely flowers," all is tinged with sadness; "the trees, the buds, the stream / Sing forth so joylessly," and when she plucks "a primrose young and pale," then casts it away "to die and wither there," she is moved to tears by the contrast between the living flower and its withered form (50). Living nature's unchanging loveliness renders her own inner changes even more unbearably apparent:

> And why are all the beauties gone
> From this my native hill?
> Alas! my heart is changed alone:
> Nature is constant still. (50)

Having established this sense of human life's inconstancy in the face of nature's constancy so early in her poetry, Anne Brontë often returns to such imagery as she explores similar feelings in later work.

In "Lines Written at Thorp Green," the forlorn poet's voice celebrates the flowers of summer—"And these bright flowers I love so well, / Verbena, rose and sweet bluebell" (80)—whose brightness is dimmed by juxtaposed death and ice images. The focus shifts from "a wild blast whose icy dart / Pierces and chills me to the heart" (79) to the flowers in the next stanza, remembered in their simple immediacy, and then shown drooping and dying like the "thick green leaves" which "must fade / And every one decay" (80). Similarly sorrowful corrections to a beautiful vision of nature are expressed in "The Bluebell," where the poet initially asserts the "sweet feeling" and power ("more or less") in little flowers:

> A fine and subtle spirit dwells
> In every little flower,
> Each one its own sweet feeling breathes
> With more or less of power.
>
> There is a silent eloquence
> In every wild bluebell
> That fills my softened heart with bliss
> That words could never tell. (73)

Delighted by the bluebell's evocative eloquence, the poet goes on to picture a sunny day in a landscape defined by the "fair" sea, a "lofty hill," and a bank where "a little trembling flower, / A single sweet bluebell" causes surprisingly "bitter feelings" of mourning in the recollection of "happy childhood's hours" (74).

These flower images express the poet's capacity to re-experience fond memories with intense pleasure which is quickly tinged with the sorrow of lost youth or lost love. Another sequence of blooming and dying occurs in "An Orphan's Lament," which chronicles the passage of time over two years of loss:

> The flowerets twice on hill and dale
> Have bloomed and died away,
> And twice the rustling forest leaves
> Have fallen to decay.   (78)

To some extent this is the position set out in another Gondal poem, "Mirth and Mourning," where the poet avers, "When Nature shows the fairest bloom, / My spirit most repines" (130). This connection between flowers and yearning is explored at length in "Memory," an earlier poem written immediately after "Yes Thou Art Gone," the aching recollection of one whose "sunny smile" lies "frozen" beneath the "cold damp stone" of the church floor—"The lightest heart that I have known, / The kindest I shall ever know" (100). After the anguish of this forlorn reminiscence, flowers in "Memory" provide a welcome release by prompting happier memories of earlier times. Here the poet escapes into a reverie of happy childhood memories associated with different flowers prompted by the sight of a solitary primrose. The transports of delight suggested in "Memory" by a bouquet of remembered flowers recall the poet's joyful youth, giving a clue to the meaning of the flower image as configured in the poems and the novels. In this poem, the poet expresses the conviction that the "holy light" of innocent youth creates an unparalleled "glory" to light the childhood experience. Memory, magically preserving a vivid picture "That haloes thus the past," is the emotional catalyst, empowering poetic perception: "Sweet memory, ever smile on me; / Nature's chief beauties spring from thee" (102). As in *Agnes Grey*, the flowers evoke a movingly distant past of carefree days, their beauty enhanced by memory:

> Still in the wall-flower's fragrance dwell,
> And hover round the slight bluebell,
>   My childhood's darling flower.
> Smile on the little daisy still,
> The buttercup's bright goblet fill
>   With all thy former power.
>
> Forever hang thy dreamy spell
> Round golden star and heatherbell,
>   And do not pass away
> From sparkling frost, or wreathed snow,
> And whisper when the wild winds blow
>   Or rippling waters play.   (102)

These verses conjure up the natural world with the simplicity of a catalogue of English country flowers, echoing at the same time the intensity of Elizabethan lyric. Their sense of enchantment makes a case even more strongly for the figurative power of memory than the poet actually claims to do. Yet poems such as "The Bluebell" and "Lines Written at Thorp Green," together with this poem's reference to childhood's bitter "pangs of grief" (102), make it clear that the evocative sweetness and beauty of flowers cannot be tasted unalloyed when the poet has suffered terrible grief, the shadow of which changes not so much the way she sees as the way she experiences the natural world in her developing consciousness. Each flower's combination of loveliness and fragility is a living embodiment of life's evanescence and duality, for nature's divine perfections tend to signify their opposite in the world of man.

Throughout the poems the forlorn cry of a bereft soul echoes and re-echoes, but the cry fuses with a stoical, even passionate determination to "press forward—and prevail" (150) in these deeply searching poetical explorations of experiential paradox. Although the poet's experience shows life teaching the traveller that suffering necessarily defines each turn in the way, "the path," she maintains, is still onward and upward. The iterative image of the path is seen in such poems as "Views of Life" (from about 1845), where the twenty-ninth stanza expresses the conviction Anne Brontë held to the end of her life that "hope the roughest path can cheer" (118). Four stanzas later, she goes on to describe a road that is "rough and long" where birds and flowers offer sweet (but passing) delight, provided the traveller is prepared to pay attention to their God-given presence along the way. Following a pattern common to the philosophical poems, she couches the whole poem in the form of a dialogue on how to reconcile life's contrarieties. She asks, not altogether rhetorically,

> Because the road is rough and long,
> Shall we despise the skylark's song,
>   That cheers the wanderer's way?
> Or trample down, with reckless feet
> The smiling flowerets bright and sweet
>   Because they soon decay? (119)

Introduced by an emphatic negative (and a change in stanza form), the answer, as befits Anne Brontë's religious and philosophical vision, lies in memory and hope:

> No! while we journey on our way,
> We'll notice every lovely thing,
> And ever as they pass away,
> To memory and hope we'll cling. (119)

Path imagery such as this is more closely defined in Anne Brontë's final poems through celebrated allusions to her philosophical recognition and spiritual choice of a path she calls the "narrow way" (160). In "The Three Guides," this narrow path through a Bunyanesque landscape of contrasting allegorical features passes from enticingly "soft" floral "meads" to "hard" rocky mountains:

> Narrow the path by which we go;
> And oft it turns aside,
> From pleasant meads where roses blow
> And murmuring waters glide;
> Where flowery turf lies green and soft,
> And gentle gales are sweet,
> To where dark mountains frown aloft,
> Hard rocks distress the feet. (150)

Guided by her chosen spirit Faith, the pilgrim determines to travel a difficult road towards a celestial "home," resolutely, hopefully, journeying upward towards a better life, "How rough so'er may be / My upward road" (149). The "narrow way" is mentioned again at the conclusion to "Self-Communion," a poem Chitham regards as an important autobiographical key, its argument shaped by "sharp" images that reconcile "bubbling" hope with musing reason (194). Having established that progress on the path of life is slow, "For hard's the way I have to go" (159), the poetic dialogue presents the culminating vision of heavenly rest in a "haven fair" where those who have striven find peace. "With such a glorious hope in view," the poet rejoices but adds the customary experiential check to the mystical glory that beckons beyond life's pragmatic barriers. The haven of rest she envisions is not to be reached without striving, toiling and suffering along the way. Ultimately, in a metaphorical enactment of the transfer of divine power to the believer, the poet asserts that through God's approval the toil itself becomes the glory: "Toil is my glory—Grief my gain" (160). The pilgrim's reward is not so much in heaven as in knowing that on earth she has faithfully worked for the good on "the narrow way," in the name of a Savior whose words she calls to witness this labor:

> "Could I but hear my Saviour say,—
> 'I know thy patience and thy love;
> How thou hast held the narrow way,
> For my sake laboured night and day,
> And watched, and striven with them that strove;
> And still hast borne, and didst not faint,'—
> Oh, this would be reward indeed!" (160)

These images of laboring and holding to a difficult path apply directly to the process and the purpose of Anne Brontë's writing, particularly when she chose to deal with contentious subjects, the "unpalatable truth" she determines to speak "with the help of God" set out in her prefatory vindication of *The Tenant* (xxxix). Her labor was not only in striving to believe in a generous, forgiving, egalitarian God, but also in writing that belief, as she does, with the passionate conviction of an uncommon intelligence. The resulting dialectic between reason and feeling runs throughout her writings, creating in words the tense, sinuous lines of a philosophically inscribed "narrow way," winding between spiritual oppositions.

In "Self-Communion," Brontë describes the poetic beginnings of the child who has experienced a feeling so intense that it is inexpressible:

> Still hiding in its breast
> A Tender heart too prone to weep,
> A love so earnest, strong and deep
> It could not be expressed. (153)

This image of voicelessness, combined with iterative images of the journey through "Life's stormy cares and toils," and "this weary desert" (153), points to an implicit solution to life's cares offered by Anne Brontë both literally and figuratively in her writings: the creative process of poetic expression is the key to understanding experience. She demonstrates the liberation of the poet's soul (which is also Agnes the teacher's soul, Helen the artist's soul and demonstrably her own) by acts of creativity and faith. Brontë's choice of images for the ending of "Self-Communion" emphasizes her philosophical conclusion that the meaning of life lies in simple actions. That simply following the path is the crux, she suggests in the poetic enactment of a metaphorical journey undertaken by a resolutely independent pilgrim with the advice of hope:

> "Press forward, then, without complaint;
> Labour and love—and such shall be thy meed." (160)

The combination of labor with love as an answer to life's pain shows creativity and faith joined in one spiritual purpose—an emotional fusion, the catalyst for which in Anne Brontë's poems is usually the inspirational power of nature. Her writings frequently suggest that the pilgrim's pathway through life's "vale of tears" (152) passes through the beauty of a natural world which reveals God's love mirrored in divine creation from flowers and trees to heath and seashore.

The "sundered" tree image, which I quoted earlier, is one of many examples of nature imagery to be found in both the poetry and the fiction, where images of natural phenomena often act as metaphors for consciousness, tracing the psychological, social and spiritual development of character. Throughout Anne Brontë's novels much of the narrative tension is created by the juxtaposition of two major image clusters: images of the natural order (or natural structures) and images of the social order (or social structures). The implied movement between the separate and often opposing domains of nature and society emphasizes a thematic concern with the pull of opposites and the co-existence of dualities—restraint with freedom, creativity with stultification, and acceptance with rejection.

Yet, although Anne Brontë's poetic methods are frequently antithetical, pitting contrasting images against each other to achieve psychosocial definition, they are not the simplistic antitheses of the morality play. To see Arthur Huntingdon in *The Tenant* as Vice personified, or Agnes Grey as Charity, would be to trivialize both novels, although it has been well pointed out that Brontë gains powerful effects by creating "simple contrasts, as clear cut as those in a Morality play."[25] Even though Agnes is long-suffering and refers to herself as someone who aims for "that charity which 'suffereth long and is kind, seeketh not her own, is not easily provoked, beareth all things, endureth all things' " (*Agnes Grey* 74), her humanity is never really in doubt. Agnes, like Helen in *The Tenant*, strives towards the ideal (charity, patience, reform of the profligate), but Anne Brontë demonstrates that both characters are essentially flawed, and both are given a confessional voice which allows for a closer study of their emotional and psychological development.

In contrasting, say, the unfriendly hearth of the "grand ladies" up at the manor, with the warmth of poor Nancy Brown's cottage fire in *Agnes Grey*, or the glow of the traditional fireplace at cosy Linden Car with the empty grate at lonely Wildfell Hall in *The Tenant*, Anne Brontë indicates not only broad social differences, but also the dilemma inherent in reconciling personal needs with social expectations. Her use of metaphorical links and contrasting images involves the reader in a complex psycho-social enquiry, rather than simply offering (as some critics would maintain) a bald moral tract. Although, as Inga-Stina Ewbank points out, Anne Brontë's novels have a definite moral purpose,[26] Brontë's iterative imagery so shapes and refines the narrative, as to elevate her fiction beyond the kind of reductive didacticism seen, for example, in Hannah More's *Cheap Repository Tracts* (1803).

As she describes the sometimes great, sometimes subtle differences between images of light and darkness, rock and sand, fire and ice, land and sea, enclosed buildings and open vistas, craggy moorland and cultivated parkland, Anne Brontë simultaneously reveals the stresses and resolutions beneath the changing face of society as a whole and within her characters in particular. Because of the often oblique way in which these both contrasting and parallel images (together with the spiritual and social dualities they imply) are incorporated into the organic structure of her fiction, Anne Brontë ultimately gestures beyond actual conflict or inequality towards possible understanding and reconciliation. She succeeds in presenting to the reader an articulation of radical potential through egalitarian balance: a human order which mirrors the openness and creative power of the divinely ordained natural order.

The surface realism of Anne Brontë's novels is structurally underpinned by these interlocking symbolical elements of field and fell, house and hearth, flowers, seasons and weather. Her use of imagery is poetic, figuring forth the powerful divisions and interconnections that define the spiritual potential of separate selves co-existing in a complex human community. By focusing on image patterns in both the poems and the novels, one sees how particular images stand out as (in Agnes Grey's words) "pillars of witness" which not only mark experience but also map the writer's developing consciousness (*Agnes Grey* 154). Agnes's reference to the reconciliatory, consoling (one might say therapeutic) function of poetry contains a timely self-reflexive, metaphorical comment on the process of writing as an attempt to reconcile spirit with experience:

> I still preserve those relics of past sufferings and experience, like pillars of witness set up, in travelling through the vale of life, to mark particular occurrences.
>
> The footsteps are obliterated now; the face of the country may be changed, but the pillar is still there to remind me how all things were when it was reared.
>
> (*Agnes Grey* 154)

Anne Brontë's use of landscape, architectural, elemental and nature imagery performs a similar function in reconciling the illusory, evanescent spirit world with the solidly pragmatic "pillars" of experience.

In the subsequent chapters I concentrate on those major image patterns that function in the novels as "structural imagery" for two reasons. From the outset, Anne Brontë's use of iterative images establishes the societal and natural structures of an actual, flawed world in which her characters move and grow: this is the world which her radical vision would reconfigure. Throughout the fictional realms of her narratives, this actual world, realistically riven with inequality and dislocation but occasionally mirroring the natural equilibrium of divine creation, gestures towards a symbolical world on which the reforming, spiritual dimensions of the text are structured. Anne Brontë's image patterns, then, both offer a psychological structure and provide an artistic structure for her novels.

CHAPTER 2

Agnes Grey:
"Pillars of Witness" in "The Vale of Life"

"All true histories contain instruction," reads the opening sentence of *Agnes Grey*.[1] This pointed assertion, linking truth with history and instruction, suggests a didacticism which, as Anne Brontë is careful to demonstrate at the outset, is tempered with an "entertaining" (3) or witty analysis of social structures. She addresses the reader directly in the opening paragraph, referring to the "kernel" of truth contained in the "nut" of her "history": a history which she thinks "might prove useful to some, and entertaining to others" (3). In this way Anne Brontë sets up the authentic base for her story and indicates a cogently defined balance between art and moral utility.

The cryptic suggestiveness of the opening "nut" image works well in securing the reader's attention, and it immediately becomes clear that the self-styled honesty or directness of her writing is not to be mistaken for simplistic moralizing or lack of conceptual depth. There is more to *Agnes Grey* than a simple moral tale. After illustrating Anne Brontë's controlled style and intellectual purpose in the reference to the "instruction" contained in "true histories," the first sentence continues: "though, in some, the treasure may be hard to find, and when found, so trivial in quantity that the dry, shrivelled kernel scarcely compensates for the trouble of cracking the nut" (3). The mock self-deprecation of the nut image suggests that the metaphorical "treasure" in *Agnes Grey* will be anything but "dry" or "shrivelled." Evidently, Anne Brontë's images are meant to convey symbolic truths, and her social and moral observations are to be found inside their shells.

Within the image patterns of her narrative are subtly intertwined motifs which operate cumulatively to create progressively deeper shades of meaning. The poetic aspect of Anne Brontë's writing lies in her imagery, and here her work shares certain similarities with that of Emily Brontë. But *Agnes Grey* and *The Tenant of Wildfell Hall* differ from *Wuthering Heights* in their detailing of a spiritual passage towards a *moral* end.[2] Anne Brontë is painstakingly careful to point out in the first lines of *Agnes Grey* that her illustrations of this particular pilgrim's progress have an instructional purpose. Yet, at the same time that she presents fiction as an instructional tool, she clearly exploits the complex allusiveness of image-filled poetic language and its embodiment of feeling. The combined expressive and structural function of her imagery simultaneously gives her fiction moral and poetical qualities.

Reflected in the analytical and confessional aspects of her lyric poems, Anne Brontë's recognition of poetry as a philosophical and therapeutic record of experience is echoed in the narrative of *Agnes Grey*. At a crucial point in Agnes Grey's spiritual development, she emphasizes the mediational value of poetry when "long oppressed by any powerful feelings which we must keep to ourselves . . . and which, yet, we cannot, or will not wholly crush" (153). In the chapter appropriately entitled "Confessions" Agnes describes poetry as both "penetrating and sympathetic" and explains how she uses it as experiential analysis, to recognize and cope with life's changing patterns:

> Before this time, at Wellwood House and here [at Horton Lodge], when suffering from home-sick melancholy, I had sought relief twice or thrice at this secret source of consolation; and now I flew to it again, with greater avidity than ever, because I seemed to need it more. I still preserve those relics of past sufferings and experience, like pillars of witness set up, in travelling through the vale of life, to mark particular occurrences. (154)

The "vale of life" through which Agnes travels on her journey to self-discovery is described by the images of different houses and the spaces between them. These images of enclosed or open spaces are the metaphorical "pillars of witness" which are "set up" to mark her progress as she moves from the "old grey parsonage" (15) of home to the grander establishments of Wellwood House and Horton Lodge, and, finally, a "respectable looking house" (196) by the sea. Comparable to the settings that mark Jane Eyre's progress from Gateshead to Ferndean, the landscapes and elements which form the open spaces between the houses create the emotional atmosphere of Agnes's passage and mark the psychological and spiritual significance of each step along the way.

As Anne Brontë maps out the particular "vale of life" through which Agnes travels, the metaphorical "pillars of witness" which are used to chart her progress give greater insight into the character's consciousness than was commonly found in other works of the governess type.[3] Unlike other protagonists from governess novels of the period, Agnes Grey is not a stereotype: she expresses an egalitarian individualism which is, like the landscape of her native hills and "woody dales" (112), roundly defined. In discriminating between Agnes's vigorous enthusiasm for the freedom of the seashore and her fear of "petrifying" (103) in the dark recesses of her employers' great houses, Anne Brontë refers to natural topography and seasonal change to illustrate a major thematic concern with the boundaries and limits imposed on the captive spirit by social structures of ownership within a repressive hierarchy. Lamenting the captive spirit's plight, Anne Brontë identifies herself as a "captive dove" in the poem of the same name, and her two fictional heroines are equally represented as captives whose awareness of what lies outside their confines adds to the "despair" of imprisonment until they escape from the drudgery of a soulless existence.[4]

Characters and relationships are repeatedly given definition, then, by reference to features of external setting. The choice of weather imagery for this purpose is one which Anne Brontë shares with her sisters, particularly Emily, and, as in *Wuthering Heights*, weather patterns are carefully schematized throughout *Agnes Grey* and *The Tenant*. Chitham, after noting some of the obvious similarities between *Wuthering Heights* and *The Tenant*, remarks that these similarities "stem from common Brontë preoccupations."[5] One such preoccupation was undoubtedly the weather, which appears as a major force in the letters of both Charlotte and Anne. Anne's poignant, cross-written letter (to Ellen Nussey) shortly before her death in 1849 makes particular mention of weather patterns. Here, as in her novels, she refers suggestively to the impact of weather on the inner landscape of the psyche when she agrees that May "is a trying month," for the "earlier part is often cold enough"; but with characteristic equanimity, she asserts that experience supports her belief in a natural pattern of mitigating warmth later: "we are almost certain of some fine warm days in the latter half when the laburnums and lilacs are in bloom."[6]

Agnes Grey's relationship with her employers and with Edward Weston can be charted through clearly linked weather images. Upon Agnes's arrival at the Murrays' house, the weather assures her of an oppressively limiting, ice-bound experience. She is shown rising "with some difficulty from under the super-incumbent snowdrift," which has been deposited on her by a "most bewildering storm" (60). Suggesting the kind of perilous, snow-covered pitfalls encountered by Lockwood in the third chapter of *Wuthering Heights*, the heavy load of this snow points to the bewildering and heavily-taxing experiences which await Agnes at Horton Lodge. Agnes is trapped by her social inferiority in the Murray household, just as she is restricted in her movements by the freezing snow.

The varying intensity of Agnes's relationship with Weston is also indicated by the weather. From the "bright sunshine and balmy air" (111) which sets the mood for their happy encounter over the primroses, the weather changes to "one of the gloomiest of April days, a day of thick, dark clouds, and heavy showers" (141) when Rosalie Murray determines to "fix that man" (139), and seems to be securing Weston's interest. Again, towards the close of the novel, weather imagery emphasizes the mounting apprehension and emotional "heat" which Agnes feels when she and Weston re-discover each other, feelings which are significantly displayed in the chapter's initial focus on "the heat of the weather" (203). The emotional tension of their reunion is then effectively released when both the weather and Weston's silence break. Weston's explanatory statement, "it was not my way to flatter and talk soft nonsense" (207), and his confession of love for Agnes both take place on a day when a "thunder-shower had certainly had a most beneficial effect upon the weather" (206). Agnes's growing inner sense of calm resolution is also correlated with the change in the weather: "a heavy and protracted thunder-shower during the afternoon had almost destroyed my hopes of seeing him that day; but now the storm was over, and the sun was shining brightly" (205). In this concluding chapter, where Anne Brontë recreates a sunny inner calm after the outer storm, the mild, sunny weather acts as a metaphor for the serenity of an integrated consciousness that balances life's problems with faith. Mirroring this preoccupation with spiritual reconciliation, a comparable concern with the weather's emotional import occurs in Emily Brontë's representation of a soft wind blowing peace over the sleeping spirits at the end of *Wuthering Heights*.

Anne Brontë also uses wind imagery in *Agnes Grey* for the delineation of character. Certain figures are characterized by images of winds blowing both hot and cold, the effects of hot and cold air also defining an imbalance in particular characters and metaphorically representing forms of communication. The unseasonably cold and windy weather upon Agnes's arrival at the Bloomfield residence in September implies that winter has begun early, signifying a wintry mood which, in emotional terms, accords with Agnes's new experience. Although Agnes's spirits are high with positive expectations, Anne Brontë stresses (through the meteorological specificity of a "north-easterly wind") that the miserable weather makes the journey noticeably longer and harder to bear: "the heavy clouds, and strong north-easterly wind combined to render the day extremely cold and dreary, and the journey seemed a very long one" (16). The cold, biting wind provides emphatic metaphorical support to Agnes's experience of Mrs. Bloomfield's bitterly unwelcoming reception and also emphasizes her vulnerability as the young governess in the hands of a new employer. Mrs. Bloomfield's way of speaking to

Agnes evokes an emotional winter: she is "chilly in her manner" (17), and to her newly-arrived employee she directs "a succession of commonplace remarks, expressed with frigid formality" (17).

Anne Brontë's choice of wind imagery here combines with the physical description of Agnes to show her blighted both by the actual physical cold without and the emotional cold within. Her exposure to the "bitter wind" has left her hands "almost palsied" (18) by the numbing cold, in an enactment of the psychological chill that freezes her faculty of speech and reduces her to an inarticulate nonentity. Agnes later recalls that the few words she is able to speak are "spoken in the tone of one half-dead, or half-asleep" (17). Echoing the expression of those forlorn, imprisoned Gondal figures in Anne Brontë's poetry, Agnes's description of her impaired voice emphasizes the silencing and numbing effect of her passage to this alien place. Agnes's distress is marked by feebly self-deprecating humor: "'My hands are so benumbed with the cold that I can scarcely handle my knife and fork,'" apologizes Agnes, "with a feeble attempt at a laugh" (18). Mrs. Bloomfield's words maintain the icy imagery in an answer meant to silence the underling: "'I dare say you would find it cold,' replied she with a cool, immutable gravity that did not serve to reassure me" (18). In this metaphorical embodiment of social barriers, Agnes is emotionally left out in the cold.

Yet, moving beyond the limited emotional scope of the Gondal poems, this part of the narrative reveals Anne Brontë's wry humor. In an acutely rendered psychological representation of shame, she creates a scene where Agnes's childlike discomfort is countered by an ironic, detached perspective of the adult. She achieves this through her choice of diction: Agnes is "sensible that the awful lady was a spectator to the whole transaction" of her inept attempt to cut the tough meat (18). The elevated formality of the language that presents a powerful authority figure set against the absurdity of the situation indicates two disparate levels of experience which recreate a psychological paradox. On one level, Agnes recognizes herself as a dependent child, sitting with a fork in her fists, "like a child of two years old," grappling with her dinner; on another level, she recalls the daunting impression of authoritarian pomposity in the "awful lady" growing proportionately more grandiose as she witnesses the absurd "transaction" (18).

Anne Brontë uses this dramatization of discomfort in combination with the winter imagery to indicate Agnes's alienation from her employers, her laconic self-representation firmly contained within the context of oppression. Agnes's "palsied" hands (18) and her inability to converse refer metaphorically to the recurring theme of freedom versus restraint. Through these details, Anne Brontë demonstrates how the power of self-expression is taken away from Agnes, and her active self is held in check, prevented from any freedom of expressive action by the deadening bonds of social tyranny.

Throughout *Agnes Grey*, Anne Brontë's use of weather imagery provides an analogous commentary on characters and their methods of communication. The way in which certain characters blow hot or cold like the wind suggests their inherent distance from, or proximity to, a golden mean of spiritual balance. In her method of signifying, one feels that Brontë grasped a notion comparable to that of the redefining semiotic force within language,[7] for radical redefinitions emerge from her acute representation of the ways in which different characters communicate. Encoded in the way her characters speak or maintain silence is a wealth of information about role, power, gender and intellect. While Mr. Murray, a florid "hearty bon-vivant" (63), puffs away stoutly in his own milieu, he is almost devoid of expression when faced with a lowly female minion such as Agnes. Hatfield, too, is all expressive energy when he comes "flying from the pulpit in such eager haste to shake hands with the squire" (84), or "sweeping along like a whirlwind, with his rich silk gown flying behind him, and rustling against the pew doors" (85), but he can find barely a murmur of comfort for the impoverished family of "poor Jem" (his dying parishioner) or for a sadly troubled Nancy Brown (100-101).

What emerges from Mr. Murray's failure to communicate (other than by extremes) is a demonstration of hierarchical boundaries. Both his limits as a man and his powerful position at the head of the squirearchy are encoded in the scant greeting reserved for Agnes. This barely acknowledges her existence and offers a form of silent dismissal for that female sub-species, the governess. His "'Morning Miss Grey,' or some such brief salutation," is delivered with an "unceremonious nod" (63); whereas his "blustering" personality is known to Agnes from other sources and from the sound of his raucous laughter in the distance or his frequently voluble blaspheming against the hapless male servants. In Agnes's significant remark that she never sees him "except on Sundays," when he joins other highly-respected but similarly unsympathetic members of the community in church, Brontë points to the hypocrisy of a fixed social order.

Like Arthur Huntingdon in *The Tenant*, Mr. Murray is a representation of what Juliet McMaster calls "the masculine ethos of the Regency";[8] by setting off his meagre dialogue with the earnest governess against the rough profusion of his speech with the male servants, Brontë's rendering of this ethos is instructive. Her analysis of social structures indicates that it is not simply a question of Agnes's being culturally unworthy of his conversation: what Brontë implies is, rather, a psycho-social dysfunction on the part of Mr. Murray which prevents either rational or affective dialogue. This inability to speak the same language as their young employee places both Mr. and Mrs. Murray firmly in the old order, whereas the enlightened governess, with her concepts of equality and moral integrity, heralds a new era which is altogether foreign to the Murrays and their unquestioning ilk. Thus the only sounds to penetrate Agnes's isolated world echo an intemperate roughness which violates the gentle humanitarian values she holds dear. In *Agnes Grey*, then, the lack of meaningful dialogue between master and servant, mistress and governess, demonstrates the supposed insignificance of the "hireling" (69): in these scenes, Anne Brontë's images re-enact the voicelessness of those who do not signify within an unbalanced social structure.

This concern with the influence of social structures on forms of expression and types of character emerges again in Anne Brontë's use of facial imagery. Pointing to the thematic emphasis on balance according to a divinely ordained natural order, Brontë also delineates her characters' emotional states through her depiction of facial coloring. The ability to hide feelings with practised ease, as Rosalie Murray does, is countered in the narrative by a moral lesson on the price to be paid for artifice of any kind. When Hatfield's hot and misguided pursuit of Rosalie ends in her rejection of him, the first indication of his pain is shown in his loss of color, which implies a loss of face. In contrast, the coquette's controlled dissimulation enables her to keep her "countenance so well that he could not imagine that I [Rosalie] was saying anything more than the actual truth" (127). The effect is given further emphasis when it is reported through Rosalie's callous recollection: "You should have *seen* how his countenance fell! He went perfectly white in the face" (127).

Although such facial images are used by other novelists (such as Jane Austen and Maria Edgeworth—whose work she well knew), Anne Brontë indicates a keenly observed awareness of the blush as psychological marker. Giving a slight twist to the symbolic link between warm coloring and healthy vitality, Brontë shows some characters with heightened color as they exert an unnatural or excessive control over others. The extremely violent passions and "insensate stubbornness" of Mary Anne Bloomfield are marked by the "high colour in her cheeks" (32, 19); and Rosalie's news of her dishonest conquest is conveyed "with buoyant step, flushed cheek, and radiant smiles showing that she, too, was happy, in her own way" (126). Resonating with the moral implications suggested by earlier narrative depictions of guilty pleasure, this image of the blushing cheek recalls the unhealthy flush of "distemper" which signals Eve's downfall after she has eaten the fruit in *Paradise Lost*.[9]

In the case of Rosalie, this changing facial imagery embodies the destructive tendencies of her character and indicates how she suffers through her misuse of power. A similar embodiment of destructive energy is presented in the grim portrait of Rosalie's ill-chosen husband, whose face, "pale, but somewhat blotchy, and disagreeably red about the eye-lids," is a physiognomical map of debauchery (192). Brontë furthers the impression of their marriage's devastating impact on Rosalie through images that recollect the former vitality of the young bride:

> a space of little more than twelve months had had the effect that might be expected from as many years, in reducing the plumpness of her form, the freshness of her complexion, the vivacity of her movements, and the exuberance of her spirits. (184)

This list of Rosalie's former glories, preceded by the verbal "reducing," has the effect of a flashback which demonstrates through the syntactic shape of the sentence a measurable reduction of her vital self. Although the character of Rosalie is ultimately treated in a relatively sympathetic light, these metaphorical pointers to her physical and moral flaws unobtrusively imply the value of a thinking woman (Agnes), set against the dubious worth of one who is frivolous and unprincipled. Brontë makes this implicit comparison between the two by showing Rosalie's thoughtless actions focalized in Agnes's pained but caring reactions to her former pupil. Thus when Agnes counsels Rosalie to be a dutiful wife and a loving mother, to find "genuine affection" (194) at least from caring for her unwanted daughter, "the unfortuate young lady" (195) recognizes the "wisdom and goodness" (194) in Agnes's views but refuses to acknowlege their relevance in a life she feels is "wasting away" for want of youthful passion (193). Although clearly self-made, the thoughtless Rosalie's plight is subtly emphasized by Agnes's shrewdly ironic perspective, combined with her "heavy heart" at the young woman's tearful clinging and "intreaties," as "poor Lady Ashby" desperately begs for "consolation" from the governess

> whose general tastes and ideas were so little congenial to her own, whom she had completely forgotten in her hours of prosperity, and whose presence would be rather a nuisance than a pleasure, if she could but have half her heart's desire. (195)

Equally effective in its subtle emphasis, Brontë's use of heat imagery suggests the moral gulf between two spiritually antithetical male characters: Murray and Weston. Revealing a social paradox in her representation of these two figures, Brontë portrays Weston as the ideal of manhood, whose character emphasizes, in Winifred Gérin's words, "the silent worth of a deeply charitable nature,"[10] and exemplifies the thematic interest in spiritual balance. Weston's fiery defence of Nancy Brown's lost cat in the face of the angry Squire Murray and his gamekeeper offers an ironic comment on different kinds of emotional heat.

Supposing that Murray is "accustomed to use rather strong language when he's heated" (108), Weston explains his confrontation with the greedy landowner in words which imply that his own warmth is of a softer genus than that of the hot-tempered Murray:

> "Miss Grey," said he . . . "I wish you would make my peace with the squire, when you see him. He was by when I rescued Nancy's cat, and did not quite approve of the deed. I told him I thought he might better spare all his rabbits than she her cat, for which audacious assertion, he treated me to some rather ungentlemanly language, and I fear, I retorted a trifle too warmly." (107-108)

Placed in this context, the heat image becomes more than an indication of temperament and takes on more widely reaching social and moral implications. Clearly, Murray's heat has nothing to do with a burning concern for fellow beings, the kind of heartfelt warmth evinced by the three characters who sit discussing the incident in the gentle glow of Nancy's cottage fire. In his egalitarian attempt to redress the social balance, Weston's warmly indignant retort contrasts the "ungentlemanly" response of Squire Murray who is hotly defending his territorial rights as landowner. Murray's is the unbalanced heat of a choleric and irrational tyrant, a sign of his excess in contrast to the warm indignance of one who would challenge social inequities. Unlike the Murray family, whose unjust use of wealth and position cannot be excused, Weston represents the kind of warm character who is blameless and needs no apology. Weston's egalitarian mentality will allow the possibility of conciliation, but the squire's extreme nature and position will not. With wry significance, Anne Brontë gives Weston the final comment: "then with a peculiar half-smile, he added, 'But never mind; I imagine the squire has more to apologise for than I.' And left the cottage" (108).

Central to the middle chapter (12) in which these scenes take place is the archetypal symbol of the hearth or fireplace, the source of other kinds of "warmth." Signaled by its obviously pivotal situation in the narrative, the hearth is a key image in *Agnes Grey*, just as it is in *The Tenant*. The hearth not only recurrently defines the importance of family within Anne Brontë's scheme, but it also offers a focus for her ethical inquiry into the contradictions of a society that houses the frigid, over-indulged "superiors" in far better circumstances than those of the caring, disenfranchised workers.

Early in the novel, the warmth of loving devotion which fuels Agnes Grey's exemplary family is suggested in the reference to her parents' bond: "if she [Agnes's mother] would but consent to embellish his humble hearth, he [Agnes's father] should be happy to take her on any terms" (4). The mutual respect expressed in Agnes's parents' marriage is of primary importance in enabling them to deal with the financial misfortunes that leave their hearth humbled to the point of emptiness. Agnes recalls the family's united response to a period of ill-fortune when her father's mercantile investments are literally sunk in a shipwreck:

> then we sat with our feet on the fender, scraping the perishing embers together from time to time, and occasionally adding a slight scattering of the dust and fragments of coal, just to keep them alive.   (8)

Although short of physical heat, Agnes's family is rich in emotional warmth, and the close family ties are actually heightened by their scant rations. In the Grey family the valued commodity of warmth is "carefully husbanded" (8), and because they look after the fire (as they look after each other) the "perishing embers" of family life are kept alive.

The warm farewells of these loving people she has left at home emphasize the bleakness of Agnes's reception at Wellwood. Her "bright hopes, and ardent expectations" (13) are abruptly shattered by her discovery that Mrs. Bloomfield is not the "kind, motherly woman" (16) she hoped would meet her. Her employer is as cold and dreary as the autumn weather. Again, arriving at Horton Lodge in a snow storm that mirrors the emotional climate, Agnes discovers icy desolation, as the "kind and hospitable reception" which she naively anticipated is coolly withheld (60). The imagery stresses that this pilgrim endures a cold and "formidable passage" (59) from place to place, and her movements are not eased by any nurturing warmth from the hierarchical establishment.

The governess's enforced isolation and lowly status are immediately brought home to Agnes by the distant situation of her allotted living quarters. The bleak space reserved for her is placed away from the warm core of the house: "up the back stairs, a long, steep, double flight, and through a long narrow passage" (61). Even more suggestive of her removal from human warmth is the "small, smouldering fire" (61) whose paucity of flame offers a poignant comment on the lack of a great blaze of warm comfort to greet the solitary traveller. What awaits her is a visibly deadening, disturbingly blank "wide, white, wilderness" of the "alien" unknown (62). This inhospitable landscape suggests a winter of the soul, where her imprisoning servitude is metaphorically reinforced by the cold, cramped room, in which Agnes's spirit must smoulder like the fire until it is released and given the freedom to burn brightly.

Mrs. Murray's attitude and stance implicitly exclude Agnes from any warm acceptance. She is pictured standing by the fire, while commenting tersely on the weather and the "rather rough" (64) journey of the previous day. Brontë gives us the spatial impression of the mistress standing between the fireplace and her new governess, effectively blocking any warmth from Agnes who ruefully compares herself to a "new servant girl" accorded scant consideration (64). Agnes points out that this treatment differs markedly from the comfort or welcome offered to a newcomer by her own mother (also a "lady"), who, in contrast to Mrs. Murray, "would have seen her immediately after her arrival . . . and given her some words of comfort" (64). Within the compass of Anne Brontë's tale, however, the comfort never comes from the rich: the gentlefolk avoid gentle acts of kindness when a poor family needs help, leaving an impoverished curate to provide the consumptive laborer "poor Jem" with the life-sustaining warmth of a good fire. The worldly cleric, Hatfield, offers no help other than "some harsh rebuke to the afflicted wife," or a "heartless observation," but Weston reacts with thoughtful generosity, as Nancy Brown reports: "when he seed how poor Jem shivered wi' cold an' what pitiful fires we kept . . . he sent us a sack of coals next day; an' we've had good fires ever sin'" (101).

From Brontë's differentiation between the cottages' honest warmth and the frigidly "proper" (39) households of the ill-bred rich, emerges a trenchant dialectic that runs beneath the surface of her apparently quiet narrative. Within the "shells" of these images of the hearth and fireplace is a discussion about innate divisions in the mainstream Victorian sensibility. Contemporary belief systems incorporated a strong sense of moral endeavor within an apparently incompatible stress on material gain. The fireplace stood at the core of the Victorian home, and became a popular symbol for the sort of solid virtues and lofty idealism which are noticeable by their absence from the rich houses of *Agnes Grey*. The sustaining warmth and hearty strength associated with the hearth are more likely to be found in the humble cottages of characters such as Nancy Brown, than in the "great" houses of the Murrays or the Bloomfields. These carefully placed images reveal the radically charged perception that whereas the cottage fireside is closed to nobody, only a privileged inner circle is invited to share the manorial hearth.

Implicit in Anne Brontë's variations on the hearth motif is an indictment of society's hypocritical endorsement of two such mutually exclusive notions—that of loving one's neighbors, and that of boldly exploiting them either for personal gain or in the name of maintaining the established order. The Evangelical emphasis on duty, which was so stringent a part of Anne Brontë's consciousness, led to an awareness of the need to conform socially. Yet, a mind and heart attuned to the egalitarian doctrines of non-conformist theology could not avoid the troubling conclusion that the existing structure was dangerously riven. The hearth, as the functional heart of family life, is an effective focus for her examination of social and spiritual divisions.

After years at Horton Lodge with the Murrays, denied the nurturing warmth of the family hearth, of acceptance as an equal, of "real social intercourse" (102), or even of companionship, Agnes understandably (perhaps even inevitably) experiences an inner death. Identifying as "a serious evil" (102) the savage influence exercised on her moral consciousness by such "ignorant" (102), restrictive employers, she begins to fear for her soul:

> Already, I seemed to feel my intellect deteriorating, my heart petrifying, my soul contracting, and I trembled lest my very moral perceptions should become deadened, my distinctions of right and wrong confounded, and all my better faculties be sunk, at last beneath the baneful influence of such a mode of life. (103)

The terms "petrifying," "contracting," and "deteriorating" suggest the sort of forensic observations which might be used for scientific purposes to record the inexorable destruction of life by the "baneful influence" of blind external forces. The statement is not simply that growth is inhibited in the absence of warmth or light: what makes the imagery memorable is that these objectively distancing terms are applied to something as intensely subjective as the internal anguish of a soul in torment.

Anne Brontë does, however, make it clear that relief and sustenance can be found for the "contracting" soul (103) in the living glow of Nancy Brown's kitchen fire, where "there's room for all" (106). This openly shared fire offers a comforting respite from the artificial restraints of Agnes's almost "deadened" (103) existence in the frigid environment of the mansion house. By juxtaposition, Brontë demonstrates how Agnes's cry from the very heart she fears is "petrifying" is immediately answered in the spiritual and moral reassurance of the scene where Nancy's cat is restored to its fireside place by Mr. Weston. Both Agnes's and Weston's commitment to a truly benevolent ideal of service takes them to the heart of Nancy's predicament and to a fireside which welcomes all—regardless of rank or fortune. The conviction that all are entitled to share the fire is borne out in a series of concerned protestations, from Nancy's "Won't you come to th' fire, miss?" to Weston's "But it strikes me I'm keeping your visitor away from the fire" (107). Their love of and concern to share the fireside (specifically mentioned in Thackeray's definition of a "gentleman")[11] identify the happy trio seated by Nancy's humble fire as nobler souls. Regardless of rank, these three are clearly closer to the lofty ideals of well-bred gentility than anything evinced by the ironically styled "angels of light" (90) up at the manor.

This spatially differentiated detailing of the natural nobility to be found in the cottage as distinct from the Lodge is ironically reinforced in the narrative by references to misplaced acts of charity. Agnes specifies the ways in which the "grand ladies" misconstrue the very meaning of nobility in the shabby condescension of their pretence at charitable actions. Focusing on Rosalie Murray's hunger for a noble title, Brontë comments scathingly on the ignoble practices of those like Rosalie, who would wish to be ennobled without any true understanding of the social implications or moral responsibilities associated with privilege. Brontë's sharp recognition of the gulf between inner and outer enrichment shows the largesse distributed by the grand ladies to be entirely devoid of Agnes's genuine benevolence. The controlled outrage in Agnes's double-edged comments reveals the ladies' charity as cold indeed:

> I could see that the people were often hurt and annoyed by such conduct, though their fear of the "grand ladies" prevented them from testifying any resentment; but *they* never perceived it. They thought that, as these cottagers were poor and untaught, they must be stupid and brutish; and as long as they, their superiors, condescended to talk to them and to give them shillings and half-crowns, or articles of clothing, they had a right to amuse themselves, even at their expense; and the people must adore them as angels of light, condescending to minister to their necessities, and enlighten their humble dwellings. (90)

Adroitly emphasizing the glaring absence of fine qualities in these ladies and gentlemen, Brontë's technique of ironic signifying dwells on light images here in order to stress the darker side of privilege. The irony gains its bite from the realization that behind the conventional light imagery linking angels—or spirituality—and enlightenment lies the truth that blind hypocrisy's damaging reality is neither angelic nor enlightening. Here Anne Brontë's language figures forth the ideal of enlightened humility rewritten in scenes emblematic of humiliation. For these ladies and gentlemen, as the narrative unfolds, the hearth is manifestly lacking in heart; the fireside is not the hub of solidly virtuous, Christian family life. Instead, we see it in Anne Brontë's terms, as a focal point for the realization that behind the condescending mask of virtue lurks a material, self-serving beast.

Referring at certain points in the narrative to the beastly or brutal aspects of the aspiring gentlefolks' ways, Anne Brontë (not surprisingly) uses animal imagery. Her interpretation of the word "animal" has, however, two aspects: she shows human brutality as animal-like, belonging to a lower order of beings, yet at the same time she also allows for the acceptance of all animals as God's "creatures" (86). In one system (the natural order) all are worthy; in the other (the social order) only the powerful or the beautiful signify. From the debased value system of a class which prizes external appearance above all else comes a catalogue of worth such as young Master Bloomfield's classification of species with its inherent endorsement of cruelty: "it's a pity to kill the pretty singing birds, but the naughty sparrows and mice and rats I may do what I like with," he chillingly recounts (22). Brontë thus divides her animal imagery to illustrate two separate elements in her thinking: the general admission that all God's creatures are worthwhile, set against the inhuman beastliness of some human behavior. Agnes makes this distinction in her comments on Matilda Murray: "As an animal, Matilda was all right . . . as an intelligent human being she was barbarously ignorant, indocile, careless and irrational" (68).

The roots of a punitive social structure are suggested in the picture of ruthlessly destructive behavior which Anne Brontë presents through her references to animals. Little Fanny Bloomfield is so hopelessly overindulged that she spits in the faces of those who cross her and bellows "like a bull" (34) when she is not humored. John Murray is "as rough as a young bear" (69) to the extent that he proves to be "unteachable—at least for a governess under his mother's eye" (69). That last, almost parenthetical, comment says everything about the problems Agnes encounters with her charges. The parents pass on their debased values to their children, who, in turn, pass them on to all they meet. Tom Bloomfield's father plays an instructive role in his son's brutal treatment of the young sparrows. When young Bloomfield pulls off "their legs and wings and heads," to which savagery his father's only comment is that "they were nasty things, and I must not let them soil my trousers," the elder Bloomfield confirms sick disequilibrium in a harshly materialistic social order (22).

These implications in the animal imagery move towards a culminating sense that such unprincipled materialists as the Bloomfields are really more the embodiment of predatory animals than civilized beings. Presenting the reader with images of feral opportunism, Brontë's language demonstrates that the scene at the Bloomfield house is oddly redolent of a den of wolves: when visitors arrive, the children clamber over them like a litter of hungry cubs. As Agnes observes, "they would indecently and clamourously interrupt the conversation of their elders, roughly collar the gentlemen, climb their knees uninvited, hang about their shoulders, or rifle their pockets, pull the ladies' gowns, disorder their hair, tumble their collars and importunately beg for their trinkets" (51). Agnes's allusion to her pupils' wild antics offers a precise reference to the untamed world they embody when she sees them, in animal terminology, "quarreling over their victuals like a set of tiger's cubs" (42). Similarly, although the figure of Uncle Robson has a comic touch with his "foppery of stays," Brontë suggests that something sinister and bestial lurks about his "little grey eyes, frequently half-closed" (46). In the manner of a predator, he brings his bird-nesting "spoils" to the children, who in turn run hungrily "to beg each a bird for themselves" (47).

With some irony, in view of her own status as brood mare to a noble sire, it falls to Rosalie Murray (one of the "ignorant wrong-headed girls" [102]) to demonstrate the contrasting usage of the words "beast" and "creature," when, in the insensate prattle of a grasping coquette she crudely assesses the comparative worth of the men present at the "odious" Sir Thomas Ashby's ball. In the space of two sentences she refers to Agnes as a "good creature" and to Sir Thomas as "young, rich, and gay, but an ugly beast nevertheless" (81), a distinction which proves to have moral as well as physical implications. For Rosalie herself Brontë reserves the most unpleasant animal metaphor to express the mindless rapacity of her determination to "fix" Weston, once Agnes's devotion to him is clear, largely to prove her superior force in a crass sexual power game. Agnes falls victim to a society which keeps her powerless, while Rosalie— indulging in "excessive vanity"—relishes the freedom to enact her cruel urge to snare and enslave. Through the eyes of painful frustration Agnes sees Rosalie take on the vicious animal shape of Tennyson's "Nature, red in tooth and claw."[12] Agnes's bitter observations place Rosalie at the level of a greedy, gloating dog:

> I could only conclude that excessive vanity, like drunkenness, hardens the heart, enslaves the faculties, and perverts the feelings, and that dogs are not the only creatures which, when gorged to the throat, will yet gloat over what they cannot devour, and grudge the smallest morsel to a starving brother.
> (149-50)

Similarly revealing, the careful juxtaposition of Rosalie's urge for a noble title with her sister's allusion to horse breeding allows Brontë to illustrate the dehumanizing effects of the marriage market. She shows that Rosalie's fascination with pedigree has more to do with the breeding animal conjured up in Matilda's reportedly "shocking" reference to her "fine blood mare" (78) than it does with vigorously independent womanhood. Although Rosalie insists that her sister's use of the word "mare" is "so *inconceivably* shocking!" (79), in the same instant she launches into an inventory of the noble pedigrees present at her ball: "two noblemen, three baronets and five titled ladies!" (79). Anne Brontë's positioning of these images of "breeding and pedigree" (79) implies that Rosalie's chosen role is ultimately debasing: that of a brood mare, mated with the most prestigious sire.

Equally informative is the way people treat their animals. In complete contrast to the harsh treatment meted out to the family pets of the Bloomfield and Murray families, the cherishing care given by Nancy Brown to her cat is an exemplar of domestic harmony and affection. In an expression of mindless barbarity, Uncle Robson's favorite dogs are dealt with "brutally" (47), and Miss Matilda inflicts upon her erstwhile pet Snap "many a harsh word and many a spiteful kick and pinch" (118) before he is taken away from Agnes (who loves her "warm-hearted companion") and "delivered over to the tender mercies of the village ratcatcher, a man notorious for his brutal treatment of his canine slaves" (155). As an enactment of the brutality meted out to all lesser beings (human or animal), Rector Hatfield's treatment of the hapless terrier is a deplorably cruel reflection of the hierarchy: "Mr. Hatfield, with his cane, administered a resounding thwack on the animal's skull, and sent it yelping back to me, with a clamorous outcry that afforded the reverend gentleman great amusement" (121). The irony in "reverend gentleman" is obvious to the reader, who is by now fully aware that his conduct throughout is neither gentlemanly nor worthy of reverence,

Nancy's cat, by contrast, is her "gentle friend" (91), and the affectionate bond between them serves to confirm the gap in awareness which separates the poor cottager from her supposed moral and spiritual superiors. The cat, which is pictured lovingly "with her long tail half encircling her velvet paws, and her half-closed eyes dreamily gazing on the low, crooked fender" (91), appears in a far more sympathetic light than the man of the cloth who unceremoniously knocks her off his knee, "like as it may be in scorn and anger" according to Nancy (97). Brontë infuses with irony Nancy's comment, "you can't expect a cat to know manners like a Christian, you know, Miss Grey" (97), since the cat appears at this moment more one of God's creatures than the clergyman.

The social tensions and inequities within the "shells" of Brontë's animal images are also outlined in two distinct images of enclosed space which are established as opposing structures of consciousness at the beginning of *Agnes Grey*. A significant source of antithetical imagery in the novel, the contrast between the material confines of the large houses and the spiritual freedom to be found in humbler dwellings reinfores the novel's psycho-social commentary. This symbolic use of setting was briefly touched upon in an unsigned review from the *Christian Remembrancer* of 1857: the kitchens of Anne and Emily Brontë are, it says, "low, and tell a tale."[13] Although clearly pejorative in purpose, this little remark comes unintentionally close to defining Anne Brontë's method of fusing the outer setting with the inner world of her characters in order to advance the psychological process and, as the anonymous reviewer suspected, "tell a tale," or, as Brontë herself intended, a "true" history (3). Early on in her tale she shows that Agnes's mother is pulled toward the "elegant house," but the humble "cottage" (4) draws her in the opposite direction and wins: "An elegant house and spacious grounds were not to be despised: but she would rather live in a cottage with Richard Grey than in a palace with any other man in the world" (3-4). Although focalized in the character of Agnes's mother, this emphatic comment anticipates Agnes's own character, revealing her pragmatic but passionate consciousness linked to that of her sensible, loving mother.

From its placement at the beginning of the novel, this glimpse of a "good" woman who knows the value of a "good" man presents in miniature a set of images that figure prominently later in the narrative. The picture of contrasting spaces and the figurative meanings attached to them gives an indication of the novel's themes, and, in this way the spatial and architectural images (common metaphors for consciousness) suggest a human need to be attuned to spiritual as well as material levels of being in order to achieve inner growth or balance. The superficial splendor promised for Rosalie's coming-out ball, for example, is immediately countered by an image of a small house, a "quiet little vicarage, with an ivy-clad porch" (77), which, unlike the rich estate of her intended husband, offers Rosalie more likelihood of real fulfillment. From her instructive use of these contrasting images, Anne Brontë makes it clear that the woman who develops as a whole person does so only on the basis of self-reliance. Agnes says of her mother: "A carriage and a lady's maid were great conveniences; but thank Heaven, she had feet to carry her, and hands to minister to her own necessities" (3). Her mother's autonomy prefigures Agnes's own journey towards independence and selfhood. Emerging from the expository spatial imagery in the early part of the novel is a suggestively configured picture that indicates ongoing thematic concerns. The last glimpse Agnes has of her home as she leaves for her new life is one which shows the solid "old grey parsonage" and the "village spire" together, illuminated by a "slanting beam of sunshine" (15). This image, which shows earthly structures linked to heaven by a beam of light, indicates the spiritual pathway ahead.

Throughout *Agnes Grey* interiors are not described in detail, but their contained inner spaces delineate boundaries or limits on the corporeal if not the spiritual freedom of those who live within. The restraint on Agnes is manifestly powerful when she reveals how she has been kept effectively a prisoner in the school-room. Although it is delivered with characteristic understatement, her comment on the deliberate curtailment of her free time betrays an abusive situation which amounts to covert enslavement, couched in the language of powerlessness: "my kind pupil took care I should spend it neither there [with Nancy Brown] nor anywhere else beyond the limits of the school-room" (147). The irony of the words "kind" and "care" indicates Agnes's bitterness without laboring the point about being held captive, for it becomes clear that there is no space for any expansion of the self in a world where she has no choice.

Yet, by careful juxtaposition, Anne Brontë also points out the illusory nature of the Murray sisters' physical liberty which they flaunt at every opportunity for self-display, while Agnes is kept indoors, her person judged to be insignificant, unworthy of public space or approbation. Closely following the picture of Agnes's confinement to the school-room is a penetrating summary of what Rosalie expects from her "inauspicious match" (147) with Sir Thomas Ashby. Beneath Rosalie's catalogue of social and material advantages is Brontë's unspoken belief that inner freedom counts for far more than the feigned liberty of profligate materialism. Brontë's representation of the marriage market's psychological crux here is acute. Although Rosalie is prepared to trade marital happiness for material gain, she fears the "inauspicious" coupling with a lugubrious character whose conjugal ownership of her will be irrevocable. No amount of positive effusions about power and property can hide the underlying suspicion that she is herself property, trapped in a position of powerlessness. Beneath Rosalie's fluttering anticipation that the marriage will broaden her social horizons is the quiet dread of its restrictive finality. Brontë reveals Rosalie's ambivalence in a paragraph that opens with her looking forward to an expansion of her world:

> Rosalie was pleased with the thoughts of becoming mistress of Ashby Park; she was elated with the prospect of the bridal ceremony and its attendant splendour and eclat, the honeymoon spent abroad, and the subsequent gaieties she expected to enjoy in London and elsewhere. (147)

Later in the same paragraph, Brontë implies that despite the triumphant expectations of the bride-to-be, her world, like her courage, actually appears to be shrinking. These expressions of wealth and freedom are rapidly undercut by the negative observations that "she seemed to shrink from the idea of being so soon united" and "it seemed a horrible thing to hurry on the inauspicious match" (147). That such words as "horrified," "warnings," and "evil" follow the reference to Rosalie's pleasurable "thoughts" and "prospects" shows the disparity between any sort of spiritual "union" and the dismal actuality of the marriage market (147). In combination with the spatial and architectural imagery, this passage re-frames the double-edged maxim that walls do not a prison make. Anne Brontë's judicious use of irony suggests that the Murrays are locked into a system of self-seeking materialism which can only stifle any nascent spirituality and must ultimately prove destructive to the soul.

Through recurring imagery of roads, lanes, walls, and windows, Anne Brontë introduces the realization that, counter to any outward appearance, the Murrays' world is actually severely limited. Within that socially delimited space, various forms of emotional control heartlessly restrict the growth of its occupants in a way repugnant to Anne Brontë's egalitarian consciousness. "But why can't she read it in the park or garden?" asks an anxious Mrs. Murray, when her nubile daughter seems to be escaping the set bounds of her genteel existence by taking her book to the field, "like some poor neglected girl that has no park to walk in, and no friends to take care of her" (119-20). Here the idea of the park where the friends ironically "take care of her" suggests a curtailment of true freedom, for, unlike Agnes who is free to cross social barriers when she is allowed to go out, the Murray daughters are entirely trapped in the limiting prejudices of the landowning class. Subsequently, the contradictions in Mrs. Murray's peculiar brand of caring are fully revealed. That the maternal interest smacks more of property management than love, is attested by Agnes's reaction to the coldly commercial exchange of this ill-fated marriage. When considering Rosalie's "inauspicious match" with the ugly Sir Thomas Ashby, Agnes confesses, "I was amazed and horrified at

Mrs. Murray's heartlessness, or want of thought for the real good of her child" (147). Agnes's dismay emphasizes a maze-like confusion in social structures where human values are mixed up with property, and caring is confused with acquisition or control.

Rosalie's flirtation with Hatfield and her persistent ramblings "in the fields and lanes that lay in the nearest proximity to the road" (124) implicitly represent a flirtation with potential freedom and real life. Since she rejects Hatfield, whom Agnes believes would be far better than the sinister Sir Thomas, it only remains for her ramblings to be curtailed within the confines of yet another, grander, park—the funereal sounding Ashby Park—and an unhappy but "princely" home (195). "I'm bound hand and foot" (122), says Rosalie before her marriage, lamenting the cessation of her flirtatious activities now that Sir Thomas is on the scene, and her remark is actually prophetic. Her seigneurial aspirations, however, plainly override any rational consideration of the dreadful consequences: "I *must* have Ashby Park, whoever shares it with me" (123). With these petulant words, Anne Brontë demonstrates a fundamental absurdity in the language of acquisition, for Rosalie is evidently marrying the space rather than the man, a pathetic misprision which reveals the bride's blindness about who is actually acquiring what or whom. The desperate tone of this statement suggests that in society's upper echelons the real passion is reserved not for human feeling, but for property. Altogether the most trenchant irony is that this foolish young woman will be the possessed, rather than the possessor of all this wealth.

The difference between Rosalie or Matilda's life and that of their governess is not just the difference between riches and poverty or between advantage and disadvantage. It is, rather, the difference between mindless superficiality and a spiritually profound, intelligent consciousness. In her characterization of Agnes, Brontë offers her reader a subtle definition of individual initiative: Agnes takes charge of her own life and seizes her opportunity with gusto "to go out into the world; to enter upon a new life; to act for myself; to exercise my unused faculties; to try my unknown powers; to earn my own maintenance" (12). As with Helen Huntingdon in *The Tenant*, Agnes's road to self-realization has its "snares and pitfalls."[14] She can be kept in the schoolroom by her demanding pupils or "crushed" into the corner of the carriage where she is continually reminded of her inferior place in life, since even personal spaces are defined for her by the often thoughtless, sometimes hostile actions of her employers. "Such a nasty, horrid place, Miss Grey; I wonder how you can bear it," says Rosalie of Agnes's place in the carriage (72), and one understands that the "place" described in such terms of disgust gestures beyond the particular corner to a generally undesirable situation in society.

However, the restraints placed on the governess are (by dint of her moral and spiritual integrity) less far-reaching than those placed on her pupils. Despite her boisterous ways—she is "full of life, vigour, and activity" (68)—Miss Matilda's world is ultimately as narrow as her elder sister's, contained as it is within the boundaries of the park and the marriage market. Agnes observes that as soon as Rosalie is married off, the next hapless daughter to fall victim to her mother's matrimonial schemes is an unwilling Matilda:

> Now also she was denied the solace which the companionship of the coachman, groom, horses, greyhounds and pointers might have afforded; for her mother, having notwithstanding the disadvantages of a country life so satisfactorily disposed of her elder daughter, the pride of her heart, had begun seriously to turn her attention to the younger. (158)

Again, through the double meanings implied by the words "denied," "solace," "disadvantages," "satisfactorily," "heart," and "attention," the language in this sentence details the underlying corruption of human relations in an acquisitive society. Inherent in the subjection of women, whose role as chattels is actually upheld by mothers such as Mrs. Murray, is the sad fact that this conniving, material heart denies maternal solace to her daughters and refuses them the healthy attention they need.

In this limited, closed world, it is, then, hardly surprising that the window represents some form of release. Mary Wollstonecraft had pointed to the promise of freedom evoked by an open window in chapter 11 of *The Wrongs of Woman* in 1798, and Charlotte Brontë also gave the window a powerful place in the imagery of *Jane Eyre*, where it functions not only as an aid to looking out but also to let strong, supernatural influences into Jane's world. Similarly, in *Wuthering Heights*, Emily Brontë shows the window as a place where the boundaries between this world and the afterlife can be crossed, a place where searing truth comes into the containing structures of social intercourse and souls can depart; it is also a place where, in Virginia Woolf's comment about Emily's novel, the reader experiences a "suggestion of power underlying the apparitions of human nature."[15]

When Agnes first arrives at Horton Lodge, she views the alien scene through a window that reveals the "unknown world—a wide, white wilderness," symbolizing the *tabula rasa* of her new existence upon which the marks of her future life are yet to be inscribed (62). After her disastrous marriage, Rosalie's increasing awareness of her self-made shackles gains pointed emphasis, as she looks "listlessly towards the window" (133). By means of the window image, Anne Brontë demonstrates that in scorning her chance of a relatively fulfilled marriage only to lose herself in material bondage, Rosalie feels a loss she cannot confront. The promise of an unfettered life that beckons beyond the window is bound to confirm the dreariness of her days within: "There's no inducement to go out now; and nothing to look forward to" (133), she laments. The finality in her tone suggests that while she refuses to perceive the full import of what lies beyond the window, her complaint about the lack of future prospects contains more than a grain of truth.

Again, later in the narrative, when Agnes visits Rosalie—now Lady Ashby—freshly ensconced in her stately mansion, Agnes's seat by a "wide, open window" (186) puts her within sight of light and liberty as she looks out from a darkening and enclosed world: "I sat for a moment in silence, enjoying the still, pure air and the delightful prospect of the park, that lay before me, rich in verdure and foliage, and basking in yellow sunshine . . ." (186). Unencumbered by worldly possessions or concerns, Agnes is manifestly more at liberty to enjoy the spiritually rich prospects of an enlightened existence because she can truly see what life sets before her through the window of the soul.

Agnes's imaginative response implies that whatever is seen through the window has much to do with the heart and soul of the viewer. Thus Agnes's description of the "prospect" is suffused with a glow of inner vitality, as opposed to the "languor and flatness" and "dull, soulless eyes" (192) of Sir Thomas Ashby or the "dreary composure" (193) of his bride who openly detests him. By contrast, Agnes is a thriving, soulful character who has gained vision and meaning from her experiences. This descriptive passage, like the longer one that follows, confirms the impression that with the inner depth of loving faith (an enlightened consciousness), the life and light beyond the walls are never quite extinguished:

> The shadow of this wall soon took possession of the whole of the ground as far as I could see, forcing the golden sunlight to retreat inch by inch, and at last take refuge in the very tops of the trees. (189)

As Agnes sits by the window, looking out from Rosalie Ashby's "elegant mansion" (or prison) at the inspirational "golden sunlight" significantly retreating to the treetops, two major image clusters reveal the difference between Agnes's broadly balanced outlook and Rosalie's severely limited consciousness. These two prominent sets of images both emphasize the salutory effects of the outdoors: one is light imagery (which is paramount and which I shall examine later), and the other is nature imagery.

The curative influence of nature and the restorative effects of being outdoors resound throughout Anne Brontë's writings. In the poems examined earlier, flowers, in particular, provide a focal point for several instances of self-evaluation and healing. Floral images in different poems and passages in the novels show a sound Victorian awareness of the language of flowers and, at the same time, they are a generic representation of divine benevolence—a God-given source of strength and beauty. The poem "In Memory of a Happy Day in February" echoes this confirmation of a divine continuum which Anne Brontë identifies in nature as a whole. More specifically, in her poem "The Bluebell" she points to flowers as individual reflections of personality: "A fine and subtle spirit dwells / In every little flower," each one breathing "its own sweet feeling" that reflects the onlooker's perception "With more or less of power" (*Poems* 73). Here the bluebell offers a "silent eloquence" which speaks of Anne Brontë's own recollections of childhood freedom: "Those sunny days of merriment / When heart and soul were free" (*Poems* 74). Similarly, in *Agnes Grey* the paradoxically "silent eloquence" of flower and nature images speaks volumes about characters and their emotional states. Agnes might compare herself with a "thistle seed borne on the wind to some strange nook of uncongenial soil" (62), but what actually forms her character has more to do with the "rugged regions" (16) where she was born. Brontë explores this concept of a rugged individualism, set against the "depressingly flat" (71) preserves of the conventional establishment, in her comparison of the landscapes surrounding the great houses where Agnes, though superior in spirit, serves as a social inferior. While the Bloomfields' grounds are distinguished by a parvenu plot with a "smooth-shaven lawn" and a "grove of upstart poplars," the Murrays' park is less nouveau riche, but still "depressingly flat to one born and nurtured among the rugged hills" (71) of "the north of England" (3).

Anne Brontë pointedly structures this grand but uncongenial setting to demonstrate how Agnes experiences the unnerving effects of social imbalance, enacted through elitist attitudes in the "tyranny and injustice" (73) of her young charges and the social isolation imposed on her by their unfeeling snobbery. Their refusal to acknowledge her presence is an attempt to dehumanize her, to reduce her to a "vacancy" (111). But Agnes resolutely refuses to accept her invisible status and finds confirmation of her own individual worth (and emotional warmth) in the beauties of the hedgerows. She escapes from her enforced position of servitude by concentrating on the flowers: "along the green banks and budding hedges . . . my spirit of misanthropy began to melt away beneath the soft, pure air and genial sunshine" (112).

Agnes's longing for some familiar visual link with her childhood—"some familiar flower that might recall the woody dales or green hill-sides of home" (112)—is gratified by the sight of the primroses: "At length I descried, high up between the twisted roots of an oak, three lovely primroses, peeping so sweetly from their hiding place that the tears already started at the sight" (112). This poignant response is a silent recognition of her own vitality and "sweetness" which she is forced to suppress in her lonely drudgery. It is also a tearful acknowledgment that the cheerful spring flower, like the primrose in "Verses by Lady Geralda" or the flowers in "Lines Written at Thorp Green," recalls a certain confidence and youthful promise which Agnes now feels is blighted. Mr. Weston's role in reaching up to gather the primroses is also deeply symbolic because in one gesture he is restoring to Agnes both the freedom of her lost youthful self and her hope for the future.

According to Victorian flower lore, these dual symbols of Agnes's past and future—the oak and the primrose—represent strength, youth, and love's doubts and fears. Traditionally, the primrose image has an ambiguous meaning. In her book *Flower Lore* (1879), a Miss Carruthers of Inverness (*sic*) wrote that the primrose is associated with "modest unaffected pride" (201).[16] But one of several meanings is also "early youth," given in Kate Greenaway's *The Illuminated Language of Flowers* (1884), offering another interpretation of the primrose image with which Anne Brontë would have been familiar.[17] As far as *Agnes Grey* is concerned, the choice of image is particularly appropriate. The floral allusion to youth parallels Agnes's own yearning for the open spaces of a happy, unfettered childhood, and the reference to a flower which conveys both pride and modesty accords with the tenacity which attends the primrose's (and Agnes's) ability to survive the more inhospitable reaches of icy heath and moorland.

This association with tenacity, rugged isolation, and sweetness, signified by the wildflowers preferred by both Agnes and Mr. Weston, indicates shared characteristics of tenderness and independence. That the flowers are guides to character is borne out in flower language when Mr. Weston questions Agnes about violets—which mean "steadfastness" according to Miss Carruthers (204) or "modesty," "faithfulness" and "watchfulness" according to Greenaway (56). Agnes, surprisingly, denies having any connection with violets: "I have no particular associations connected with them, for there are no sweet violets among the hills and valleys round my home" (113). Her favorite flowers are "Primroses, blue-bells, and heath-blossoms," which signify early youth, constancy, and solitude (Greenaway, 48, 22, 34). Agnes's curious dissociation from the "sweet violets" indicates something of her rugged background and suggests that Brontë's heroine is no shrinking violet; nor is she modestly, faithfully, watchful (which implies dependency): once her painful obsession with Edward Weston is overcome, Agnes turns away from watchful dependence towards a solitary path, where she strives for autonomy and self-sufficiency.

Unlike her pupils, Agnes exhibits a plain, simple honesty (suggested by her love of wild flowers) which counters the manipulative dishonesty indulged in by Rosalie Murray in the course of her amorous adventures. When Rosalie is playing her calculated game of dalliance with Mr. Hatfield, she is shown holding a sprig of myrtle—traditionally carried as a symbol of love by a bride in her wedding bouquet. However, Anne Brontë uses this floral emblem with an ironic twist to reveal Rosalie's superficiality, for she is clearly unaware that there is any meaning attached to it other than an entirely frivolous one: "a graceful sprig of myrtle, which served her as a very pretty plaything" (120). The image of the brideflower as plaything indicates that love—in the sense of mutual respect and caring—has no serious place in the life of someone like Rosalie: nubile sweetness is just another piece in a power game which allows her vanity to be gratified at the expense of others. An even more overt demonstration of her foolishness is presented in Rosalie's final reaction to her abject suitor, Hatfield: she impatiently gives the myrtle away with a toss of her head, metaphorically tossing away the opportunity for loving reciprocity in a marriage of equals. Even though she recognizes Hatfield's worth as superior to the "ugly" rake Sir Thomas Ashby, she is adamant that "poor Mr. Hatfield" (122) could never be a serious contender for her acquisitive "preference" because his income barely amounts to seven hundred a year: "I never should forget my rank and station for the most delightful man that ever breathed. . . . Love! I detest the word! as applied to one of our sex, I think it a perfect insult" (122). Rosalie's misunderstanding of the word "love" demonstrates figuratively the blind materialism that confuses superficialities with true meaning and restructures lives according to the empty reckonings of commercial exchange.

In contrast to the mindlessness of Rosalie—who presents a perfect foil to the character of Agnes—the profoundly sensitive, Christian consciousness of Agnes is conveyed through images of light and shade. A conventional metaphor for consciousness, light here conveys the brightly transcendent potential of a love that reflects the divine presence, showing Agnes linked to the higher ideal. As the representation of a caring, spiritual person linked to the ideal of receiving God's love and the responsibility of dispensing that love to those she meets in life, Agnes takes the idea of love (both in its sacred and profane senses) very seriously. The confirmation of a "divine truth" identified by Anne Brontë in light generally is echoed in the poem "In Memory of a Happy Day in February":

> It was a glimpse of truths divine
> Unto my spirit given
> Illumined by a ray of light
> That shone direct from Heaven! (*Poems* 82)

Light also as a symbol for love and hope is a poetic staple, but Brontë's psychologically probing language, as she examines Agnes's developing consciousness, imparts a compelling spiritual inquiry to the interplay of light and shade.

As Agnes Grey struggles to reconcile her anguish at the lack of human love in her life with her spiritual beliefs, her mind is so numbed by loneliness that she can no longer see the heavenly light. Her wearisome isolation causes her to become unbalanced and fearful that the light of spiritual inspiration is virtually clouded out: "the gross vapours of earth were gathering around me, and closing in upon my inward heaven" (103). In her troubled state Agnes is earthbound, and Brontë shows that Agnes's preoccupation with her earthly love for Mr. Weston forces her (like the stifling Earth spirit in "The Three Guides") to lean dangerously in the direction of an obsession: "And thus it was that Mr. Weston rose at length upon me, appearing like the morning star in my horizon, to save me from the fear of utter darkness" (103).

Towards the end of the novel, when faced with the loss of her love, Agnes finds it hard to relinquish the spiritual sustenance she has derived from him. Weston has become the only "bright object" on a gloomy horizon: "How dreary to turn my eyes from the contemplation of that bright object, and force them to dwell on the dull, grey, desolate prospect around, the joyless, hopeless, solitary path that lay before me" (155). Central to this embodiment of depression, however, is Anne Brontë's point that Agnes has sufficient intelligence to recognize how her desperate need—"a painful troubled pleasure, too near akin to anguish"—is unhealthy enough to be "evil," for it hinders true development and effectively keeps her in "fetters" (155). She is also given the foresight to comprehend that she cannot progress until this "troubled pleasure" is relinquished, allowing the total experience of a solitary life. Like Jane Eyre, who also determines to follow a solitary path after wrenching herself away from Rochester, Agnes experiences a profound insight, seeing the fullness of wisdom intervene and guide her away from spiritual destruction: "It was," Agnes perceives pragmatically, "an indulgence that a person of more wisdom or more experience would doubtless have denied herself" (155). Agnes learns to walk the "solitary path" (155) with joy and hope before she is finally enabled to join Mr. Weston.

Part of this learning process puts Agnes into the deeply contemplative state we see when she sits at Rosalie Ashby's window. The dismal lethargy into which she has sunk calls forth one of the more purple passages in the novel, and Brontë's writing here carries an air of spiritual hiatus which is emotionally fitting at this point in her heroine's development. Again, the light and shade images are crucial:

> The shadow of this wall soon took possession of the whole of the ground as far as I could see, forcing the golden sunlight to retreat inch by inch, and at last take refuge in the very tops of the trees. At last, even they were left in shadow—the shadow of the distant hills, or of the earth itself; and, in sympathy for the busy citizens of the rookery, I regretted to see their habitation, so lately bathed in glorious light, reduced to the sombre, worky-day hue of the lower world, or of my own world within. For a moment, such birds as soared above the rest might still receive the lustre on their wings, which imparted to their sable plumage the hue and brilliance of deep red gold; at last that too departed.
> (189)

What stands out in this passage, apart from the rather florid prose, is that the shadows of structures (such as walls and buildings) are shown to have taken "possession" of the open spaces and to have obliterated the sunlight. Agnes is "observing the slowly lengthening shadows from the window," in such a way as to suggest that her vision of social constrictions is gaining clarity. As the imagery here implies, she must move away from earthly entrapments and the danger of being "possessed" by the shadows of earth, towards a higher, more enlightened spiritual plane.

The use of dramatic coloring or *chiaroscuro* in this verbal picture succeeds in evoking Agnes's spiritual dilemma. Anne Brontë highlights the darker brush strokes (suggesting both Agnes's and Rosalie's blighted dreams) with lustrous touches which imply a stubborn spark of hope gleaming only in the eye of the believer. The elongated vowel sounds recall arcs of flight (Agnes's flights of fancy) and the encroaching shadows correspond with Agnes's increasing awareness that her dream of a life with Mr. Weston must be allowed to fade in the realism of "the sombre, worky-day hue of the lower world."

Yet at this climactic moment, she still retains a glimpse of something "so lately bathed in glorious light" that promises a glimmer of hope for the future. As Brontë shifts her focus from the contemplative person within to the busy scene without, she develops a tension between movement and inaction, introversion and extroversion, thought and deed. We are left with the suspicion that, unlike Rosalie Ashby whose active self has been obscured by the shades of materialism, Agnes will not opt for a passive role: she will resolve her dilemma by actively stepping out of a "quiet, drab-colour life" (189), and reaching for the higher ideal, she will be liberated like one of the birds that soars above the rest to catch the closing brilliance of the day.

An interpretation such as this accords with Anne Brontë's own beliefs, and within the context of her religious philosophy it is perhaps predictable that Agnes must make peace with her Maker before she can progress much further. Yet, the description of Agnes's epiphany is not simply given in limited religious or moral terms. Deeply religious though she was, Anne Brontë gives us an inspirational view of more than the godhead revealed in nature. She also shows us selfhood discovered in a way that echoes the radical affirmation of feminine selfhood proposed by Mary Wollstonecraft fifty years earlier: Agnes is presented primarily as a complex person who is finally put in touch with all aspects of herself.

As in *The Tenant*, the image of the sea reflects this limitless personal potential. The sea represents an agent of liberation for Agnes, who finds release in its ceaseless, unrestrained activity: "it was delightful to me at all times and seasons, but especially in the wild commotion of a rough sea breeze" (196). Agnes's expansive world, with its sea breezes and freedom beyond time or season, is an instructive contrast to the incarceration of Lady Rosalie Ashby in her elegant mansion where the lifeless, material images speak of passing time and death.

Compared with the "delightful" dynamism and freedom of the seashore (shaped by "foaming and sparkling" waves, "dimpled pools, and little running streams" [197]) where Agnes is liberated, Rosalie's surroundings are dully limited, joylessly defined by static objects and oppressive walls. Within the "splendid house and grounds" for which Rosalie has bargained away her life, having coveted it "whatever price was to be paid for the title of mistress" (181), she is surrounded by conspicuous materialism with "many elegant curiosities" (185) but is altogether lacking in love. She cynically estimates her baby girl's place in all this as "only one degree better than devoting oneself to a dog" (194). Confirming the inherent imbalance of this position, the young mother's "melancholy sigh" signifies the fruitlessness of her acquisitive existence, "as if in consideration of the insufficiency of all such baubles to the happiness of the human heart, and their woeful inability to supply its insatiate demands" (186). This blind obeisance to things—"baubles," as Agnes comments in the reductive language that shows Anne Brontë's own snort of disapproval (186)—again shows Rosalie to be less the possessor than the possessed; she is clearly owned by her own vapid materialism. The marble busts that surround her are metaphors for truncated, captive selves, captured in cold, white stone, while the little timepiece and "little jewelled watch" (186), which Rosalie ironically shows Agnes with unknowing "animation," mark the empty passage of her wasted life.

This sterile, soulless world presents the antithesis to Agnes's now sunny, purposeful life. Juxtaposed against these interior scenes of Rosalie's suffocating union with a man she detests are Agnes's seaside escapades, in which her healthy delight in autonomous action identifies her as a woman free from the bondage of dependency. Unlike Rosalie Ashby, Agnes no longer needs a man to validate her existence; she becomes fully self-actualized. Signalling the transformation from a "drab-colour life" (189) which oppresses Agnes at Ashby Park, the imagery in the later seascape radiates light and color. "No language can describe," writes Anne Brontë, although she succeeds in doing so admirably,

> the effect of the deep, clear azure of the sky and ocean, the bright morning sunshine on the semi-circular barrier of craggy cliffs surmounted by green swelling hills, and on the smooth, wide sands, and the low rocks out at sea—looking, with their clothing of weeds and moss, like little grass-grown islands—and above all, on the brilliant, sparkling waves. (196-97)

These images of light bouncing from the different tactile surfaces of sea to shore and back again recreate the electrifying vitality of a divinely empowered life force. Seen through Agnes's eyes, the scene on the sands is sparkling with sunlight and bursting with energy, its expansive vigor indicating her own expanding sense of self. This liberating energy creates a peculiarly balanced environment: "Just enough heat to enhance the value of the breeze, and just enough wind to keep the whole sea in motion, to make the waves come bounding to the shore, foaming and sparkling as if wild with glee" (197). Through the repeatedly modified images of heat and wind, with the boundless action of the living waves below—reflecting "brilliant" light—Brontë's imagery allows the reader to experience a divinely balanced still point at the center of motion, a Miltonic echo of creation's "bright essence."[18] Both Agnes and the personified waves embody the effervescent "glee" of a being who has finally broken free from shackles; Agnes has become an empowered entity, a vital person in her own right.

Appropriately, this transcendent state occurs in solitude, when "nothing else was stirring—no living creature was visible besides myself"

(197). As well as the suggestive Miltonic echoes of creation in these images, Agnes's psychic rebirth is also likened to the birth of Aphrodite from the waves. The sense that the sea becomes a source of spiritual renewal is reinforced also by the early morning setting, with the pristine beauty of a freshly renewed landscape: "My footsteps were the first to press the firm, unbroken sands:—nothing before had trampled them since last night's flowing tide had obliterated the deepest marks of yesterday, and left it fair and even" (197). At this point Agnes is not only physically refreshed but spiritually transfigured, feeling as though she had wings on her feet and "could go at least forty miles without fatigue" (197). The euphoria of her self-discovery gives her courage to venture out onto the slippery rocks where she is poised on a "little mossy promontory" (197), surrounded by a sea of living water. Similarly, when Edward Weston proposes to her, they are symbolically poised on the edge of a precipice, from which they watch "the splendid sun-set mirrored on the restless world of waters" at their feet (208). Their union, unlike that of the ill-matched Ashbys, is demonstrably blessed when it is defined by all these profoundly resonant images of power and creation.

In these contrasting scenes, language evokes seasonal change, and image perfectly mirrors the psychological development of character. The correspondence between the outer landscape and the inner life of Brontë's characters is of paramount importance in her writing. Throughout *Agnes Grey* imagery of nature and open spaces reflects the successive stages through which Agnes passes as she moves from the rugged hills of her childhood, through the "depressingly flat" spaces of her governess years, to the personal high point on that sea-cliff which affords a prospect of creative union in the fulfilment of marriage to her equal. Countering the images of buildings and their lifeless contents, images which relate to nature and open spaces add a spiritual dimension to the narrative; together, they act as "pillars of witness," testifying to the actualization of Agnes's escape from social degradation and the "indignities" (74) which limit her existence in the socially structured establishments where she serves.

Admittedly, *Agnes Grey* is restricted in focus, concerned as it is with the psychological development of one main character within the scope of Brontë's original title for the novel—*Passages in the Life of an Individual*, mentioned in her birthday note of 31 July 1845. Yet it has a textual richness which could be identified as a peculiarly feminine grasp of "the intricacies of personal relationships" (as Ian Watt says in his analysis of the supremacy enjoyed by the woman novelist). Such psychological acuity combined with moral vision places Anne Brontë firmly within the literary heritage of other great women writers such as Mary Wollstonecraft, Ann Radcliffe, Maria Edgeworth, Frances Burney, and Jane Austen.[19] Anne Brontë's bold analysis of realistic relationships through interconnected poetic images exemplifies an elaborately structured and affectively subtle technique which reveals her as a writer who was ahead of her time. Robert Barnard's comparison of her writing with that of her sisters contains the lucid observation that her work "looks forward," and he places her at a literary crossroads that leads towards psychological and social realism.[20]

In *Agnes Grey* Anne Brontë's technical achievement lies in the creation of a closely-woven textual fabric, the apparent simplicity of which is deceptive. With this first novel, she does not explore the more complex turns of plot or dramatic enigmas that shape her sisters' works and that are to give the dimension of instructive parody to *The Tenant*.[21] The "instruction" promised at the beginning of *Agnes Grey* is present in both novels, but the narrative development of *Agnes Grey* shows a straightforward approach which accords openly with its plainly stated moral purpose. But, while the "quietness" and "realism" of this direct method are important,[22] Anne Brontë's achievement in *Agnes Grey* goes beyond a simple representation of scenes from a life; her keenly rendered psychological enquiry is powerful in its quiet intensity. From the cryptic thoughtfulness of the opening nut metaphor to the succinct finality of its closing statement, "And now I think I have said sufficient" (208), *Agnes Grey* combines an intentionally straightforward style with iterative images that both entertain and instruct. In addition to setting the novel's boundaries of restraint, the two framing statements indicate the formal structure of the text and provide an ideal vehicle for exploring major themes of balance and imbalance, oppression and liberty, restraint and growth. Terry Eagleton's perception accurately characterizes the final line of *Agnes Grey* which, in his words, "neatly captures the laconic modesty of the whole, the sense of a work attractively reserved in feeling without any loss of candid revelation."[23]

This reserve is both a stylistic and thematic feature of Anne Brontë's work. The apparent stillness of her writing, compared with that of her sisters, is not, however the stillness of creative timidity or inarticulation. One image from late in the novel effectively answers the plethora of critical suggestions that her writing lacks power. Her reserved but poetic style bears comparison with the calm but not inactive surface of the sea, above which Agnes stands on her "mossy promontory" (197), exulting in the contained power and unseen depths of the tidal water:

> and then I turned again to delight myself with the sight and sound of the sea dashing against my promontory—with no prodigious force, for the swell was broken by the tangled sea-weed and the unseen rocks beneath; otherwise I should have been deluged with spray. (198)

Life imitating art in this instance, the experience of the reader parallels the experience of the heroine who turns again to delight herself with the sensory impressions of the scene. The reader does not emerge from the sight and sound of Anne Brontë's narration "deluged with spray," but one is left with an abiding sense of its assiduous swell—of intertwined image patterns embedded beneath and controlling its surface movement.

Yet, Brontë's method is an entirely self-conscious one, as can be seen from carefully placed authorial statements referring to form and content. These have, moreover, a dual function. First, the self-reflexive comment mid-way through the narrative, "Had I seen it in a novel, I should have thought it unnatural" (149), together with repeated references to the "benefit" (36) or "patience" (36, 63) of the "reader" (63, 146) and the "prolixity" (36), "prosing" (146), "reflections" (146), "design" (36) or "arguments" (146) of the writer, combine to undermine the separation between narrator and story, drawing the reader into the fictional world. This effectively questions the borderline between reality and fiction, giving the impression of lived personal experience which supports the novel's didactic, moral purpose. But such comments also testify to an awareness of the writer's rhetorical method and the careful underpinning of theme with image, a deliberate artistry which conjoins poetry with moral instruction and is the structural base of her style. In Anne Brontë's ordering of thematic motifs within the interlocking image patterns of structural imagery one finds every sign of the unobtrusively crafted textual fabric which George Moore saw as "simple and beautiful as a muslin dress."

CHAPTER 3

The Tenant of Wildfell Hall: From Hearth's "Desperate Calmness" To Heath's "Loftiest Eminence"

With characteristic bluntness, Anne Brontë declares in her preface to the second edition of *The Tenant of Wildfell Hall*: "If I can gain the public ear at all, I would rather whisper a few wholesome truths therein than much soft nonsense."[1] This decision to tell "a few wholesome truths" about such unwholesome subjects as infidelity, brutality, and drunkenness, and to do so in "unpalatable" (xxxix) detail, was one that damaged Anne's reputation in the eyes of those she calls "the most fastidious" of her critics (xxxviii), not least of whom was her sister Charlotte.[2] Writing to W. S. Williams on 31 July 1848, immediately after the novel's publication, Charlotte Brontë expressed stifling disapproval of its subject matter: "for my own part, I consider the subject matter unfortunately chosen—it was one the author was not qualified to handle at once vigorously and truthfully."[3] Charlotte Brontë's subsequent refusal to allow Smith, Elder & Co. to reissue *The Tenant* after her younger sister's death temporarily silenced Anne's poignantly honest voice, but the truthfulness and vigor which Charlotte found lacking in *The Tenant* are the very qualities which have kept it alive.

Even at first sight, *The Tenant* resounds with radical vigor and penetrating authenticity. The discrepancy between Charlotte Brontë's opinion and the novel itself says more about the sisters' different approaches to writing fiction than it does about their relationship. From the opening letter, which reflects on the business at hand—"story-telling" (5)—Anne's deliberately controversial tale grips the imagination and presents a purposeful articulation of social and psychological conflict. *The Tenant* overturns the initial allusion to an "old world story" (6) by offering in its place a searching reappraisal of orthodoxy.

The Tenant maintains the same moral intent expressed in the opening of *Agnes Grey*, but the organization of its material is more complex. Structural imagery—the underpinning of theme with interlocking image structures—has a comparable function to similar imagery in the earlier novel, but it is developed to explore the broader scope of *The*

Tenant. In order to tell her "honest" (xxxviii) story, and avoid lessening its impact with any "soft nonsense" (xxxvii), Anne Brontë chose a direct, confessional method similar to that of *Agnes Grey*, but the first-person narrative in *The Tenant* is incorporated into a more intricate tripartite structure, each part of which varies the narrative point of view. The text is set out in the epistolary form, but it is given an added dimension in the representation of the middle section as a diary, reported (but not written) by the writer of the framing letters, who—like Lockwood in *Wuthering Heights*—is a male narrator. As Naomi Jacobs points out, the reader thus approaches the diary's female story, a "horrific private reality," through a deliberate displacement of the framing "perceptual structures" offered by this significantly male narrator who represents the familiar, official world that attempts to frame or cover the reality of domestic violence.[4] After the relatively simple chronology and straightforward plan of *Agnes Grey*, this more complex, varied design certainly demonstrates Anne Brontë's artistic growth and her willingness to experiment with her medium.

As a means of adding veracity and dramatic force to her narrative, the epistolary framework, with its enclosed account of Helen Huntingdon's marriage (written from Helen's point of view), is psychologically effective. A singular lack of critical insight must have prompted George Moore to suggest that "almost any man of letters" would have redirected the author's path away from the use of the journal or diary towards a more conventional exchange of confidences in "an entrancing scene" of dialogue.[5] Fortunately, no man of letters was shaping Anne Brontë's secretly radical vision. Clearly, the facile painting of such an "entrancing scene" of dialogue would not only be at variance with her decision to tell "an unpalatable truth" and to do so from the heart, but it would also miss an opportunity to explore a form of covert female authority in the journal. Brontë clearly recognized the personal diary as a potentially subversive expression of women's experience, its forbidden authority offering the sole outlet for those imprisoned by repressive social structures. Intellectually, she perceived a less obvious path than that offered by Moore: one which led her to break away from the patrimony of literary predictability.

In *The Tenant*, Anne Brontë unerringly grasped the radical implications of allowing her heroine to speak for herself within the thoughtful confines of the written page. The sentimental or discursive limits of Helen's tale thus told intrinsically give it greater psychological scope. More than any sentimental scene, the diary of a woman driven slowly but surely to desperation and flight makes potent reading and presents a searching analysis of abusive patriarchal attitudes and authoritarian tactics. Clearly, in her choice of method Anne Brontë recognized the greater impact of revealing the disintegration of the marriage from the inside, as it occurs, in an intricate process of observation and sensation mediated by the secret history of abuse. This "woman of letters" astutely perceived the necessity of giving her heroine the more powerful tool of the pen rather than allowing her mere pretty speeches.[6]

Here the diary functions doubly as part of the narrative structure and an element of structural imagery in itself. It suggests different levels of meaning: like Helen's painting, it represents her urge for creativity within a closed environment, and, like the open spaces inscribed within the paths and roads leading away from Grass-dale to the windy heights of Wildfell, the written pages of the diary signify Helen's escape route. The seductively candlelit diary, which a captivated Gilbert Markham pores over until daybreak, contains an implicit statement about the empowering process of authorship. An example of reflexive literary technique within the novel, the diary also emblematizes interconnected levels of expression in its fusion of narrative form with figurative meaning, a kind of *mise en abyme* or book within a book, which gives *The Tenant* the psychological perspective or "depth beyond depth" identified by A. Craig Bell.[7]

This depth is achieved largely through Anne Brontë's choice of dominant image patterns. As in *Agnes Grey*, images of contrasting architectural structures outline the different directions in which characters move and grow. In *The Tenant*, the more controversial examinations of conflicting states, such as fidelity and infidelity, sobriety and drunkenness, marital unity and estrangement, are sharply defined by the greater contrasts between buildings and their surrounding countryside. Wildfell Hall is an extreme example of isolation and elevation as it stands on the "wildest and loftiest eminence" (18) in symbolic union with its tenant, who is a combination of wild unconventionality, lofty virtue, and eminent intelligence. Linden Car, on the other hand, is tucked away safely in the valley and is described chiefly through images of its cosy social gatherings or the conventional "gleam of a bright red fire through the parlour window" (7). The obvious distance between the two environments underlines the gulf between the estranged, marginalized tenant and the unified, conservative social group that judges her by the very standards she questions. Although it is not directly connected with the picture of Helen's marriage, comfortable Linden Car outwardly sets a tone of conventional family unity which, however, is undercut by its own reliance on the subjection of women. These underlying inequities are then dramatically reinforced by comparison with the overtly painful divisions and immoral abuses that hold sway at Grass-dale.

This double-edged interplay of dualities and shifting meanings can be seen throughout the text. In such scenes as the following encounter between Helen and Gilbert, contradictory impulses work in unison to produce a figurative density which demonstrably repudiates Terry Eagleton's comment on "the slightness" of Anne Brontë's fiction.[8] Helen's first offering of a rose to Gilbert Markham in the tenth chapter, "A Contract and a Quarrel" (an appropriately antithetical heading), draws forth a rapid succession of contrasting images. These images create the visual redefinition, metaphorical cross-referencing, and psychological tension which shape the entire novel.

> Instead of taking it quietly, I likewise took the hand that offered it, and looked into her face. She let me hold it for a moment, and I saw a flash of extatic brilliance in her eye, a glow of glad excitement on her face—I thought my hour of victory was come—but instantly, a painful recollection seemed to flash upon her; a cloud of anguish darkened her brow, a marble paleness blanched her cheek and lip; there seemed a moment of inward conflict,—and with a sudden effort, she withdrew her hand, and retreated a step or two back.
> "Now Mr Markham," said she, with a kind of desperate calmness, "I must tell you plainly, that I cannot do with this." (88)

To the extent that the oxymoron describes a pull in opposite directions, the choice of the phrase "desperate calmness" not only describes Helen's attitude adroitly, it also offers a holophrastic clue to the novel's radical controversiality. Stating in her Preface the desire to "give innocent pleasure" and her duty "to speak an unpalatable truth" (xxxix), Anne Brontë sets up a process that blends the ironic, reforming urge of satire with the plain-speaking simplicity of a confessional "true" story. The polemical basis of her intent is fully realized in her method of pitting images against each other: Gilbert Markham's description of Helen demonstrates how the "flash" and "brilliance" rapidly give way to the shades of "cloud" and darkness; the extended hand is countered by the withdrawn hand, and the colorful "glow of glad excitement on her face" is undone by "a marble paleness." George Moore's admonitory reading of the novel missed the point, in that none of this is meant to be "entrancing"; for Anne Brontë's writing is intentionally seditious. Her coloring of the literary canvas throughout demonstrates a knowing application of *chiaroscuro* to achieve sharp psychological definition of subject, while her imaginative exposure of society's moral failures puts her in the milieu of Augustan social satirists such as Delarivier Manley and Swift. The definition of social mores achieved in *The Tenant* is both disturbing and revelatory.

Brontë's characterization has been slighted by Phyllis Bentley as "often either feeble or crude," but through the suggestive use of iterative image schemes, the characters in *The Tenant* evolve effectively during the course of the narrative.[9] Closer to my reading of Anne Brontë's method, A. Craig Bell identifies a "time-sense," by which "unique" feature the major characters, Helen and Gilbert (to a lesser degree), "emerge from their emotional stresses and trials subtly different."[10] It seems to me that this continual process of redefinition is achieved in large part through the shifting meanings implied by contrasting image patterns.

With a major image scheme that switches angel and devil pictures from stoical Helen to profligate Huntingdon and back again, Anne Brontë plays on the irony of Helen's naive misconceptions about Arthur's goodness. She uses the angel versus devil motif to call attention to what becomes a kind of pitched battle of souls. The conflicting images of either angelic or demonic possession form a major thematic pattern in the novel, and, combined with the contrasting settings and motifs of darkness and light, succeed in creating an undercurrent of spiritual and emotional strife. According to Inga-Stina Ewbank, "the relationship between Helen and Huntingdon gets its peculiar flavour and much of its interpretation by being developed against a tightly-woven tissue of religious references."[11] Certainly, the text is tightly woven, but Anne Brontë creates this characteristic intertwining only partly through the religious references: much of her narrative's powerful complexity is attained through an iterative antithetical image scheme that introduces archetypal symbols into its exploration of entrenched sexual divisions and social hierarchies.

Colored by such images of angels and devils, heaven and hell, Helen's validation of her physical response in spiritual terms highlights the unbalanced psyche of passion. The irrational confusion of her response is stressed by the breathless exaggeration of her comparison between repulsive Wilmot and charming Huntingdon: "It was like turning from some purgatorial fiend to an angel of light, come to announce that the season of torment was past" (143). This hyperbole only emphasizes ironically how Helen's muddled thinking fails to grasp that the reverse is true: Huntingdon's arrival on the scene announces the beginning of Helen's worst torment. In Helen's *psychomachia*, Passion clearly wins over Reason, and the more sinister side to Huntingdon's advances is recognized, but not accepted, when she says: "but I feared there was more of conscious power than tenderness in his demeanour" (143). These references to control and dependence clarify the narrative's psycho-social commentary. Underlying Helen's relationships with Huntingdon and Hargrave is a vicious power struggle (the chess game with Hargrave exemplifies the metaphorical representation of this), but Anne Brontë adds a further dimension by frequently reminding the reader of the inner battle which accompanies it. Bearing in mind this carefully laid groundwork, the sustained metaphorical and symbolical sub-structure which explores the difference between "outward seeming" and "inward mind" (121), and the obvious pull between earthly and spiritual concerns, one can hardly see how Terry Eagleton reaches the barren conclusion that "Anne Brontë's work, by contrast [with that of her sisters] knows no such conflict between the flesh and the spirit."[12]

Precisely such a conflict between flesh and spirit informs the intense discussion between Helen and Aunt Maxwell in the chapter entitled "Persistence." Helen's persistent (and natural) "flesh" prompts her to override the traditional spiritual guidance offered by her aunt. She is able to counter the biblical authority of her aunt's warning question from 2 Corinthians 6, "'What fellowship hath light with darkness; or he that believeth with an infidel?'" (177), with her own misguided contention that beneath Huntingdon's rakish exterior she recognizes his true self "shining out in the unclouded light of his own genuine goodness" (177). A more pragmatic rebuttal to Aunt Maxwell's allusion to darkness and light comes through Helen's dismissive reply: "He is not an infidel; —and I am not light, and he is not darkness, his worst and only vice is thoughtlessness" (177). Helen's defensive response here is imbued with heavy irony, for her apparent gloss of the word "thoughtlessness" as a lesser sin implicitly runs counter to the authorial meaning. Along with her prefatory message to the "young and thoughtless traveller" or the "thoughtless girl" (xxxviii), Anne Brontë's clear-sighted belief in thoughtful responsibility (likely hard-won through personal experience with Branwell's alcoholism) offers an implied rebuke to those who persist in seeing abusive men as "thoughtless" children. Rather than undermining the darkness imagery as Helen intends, this comment emphasizes even deeper differences between the two and impugns Helen's over-generous, even maternally over-protective humanity.

Having thus indicated that she is dealing with humanity divided and not simply with opposing abstractions, Anne Brontë suggests by further instances of the angel-devil motif that Helen and Huntingdon are heading in different directions. Aunt Maxwell's grim pronouncement that Huntingdon and his friends are running "down the headlong road, to the place prepared for the devil and his angels," and Helen's answer, "Then, I will save him from them [the loose friends]" (147), are combined later with richly bathetic irony in an evocative symbol of entrapment: "I made an effort to rise," says Helen, "but he was kneeling on my dress" (164). A. Craig Bell points out that this detail is also a symbol of Helen's powerlessness, but the ironic cameo of disparity embodies more than Helen's lack of power over Huntingdon.[13] The image shows her attempting to stand free of something which holds her down—not just Arthur kneeling on the trappings of her femininity, but her physical passion which, paradoxically, also allows a release of energy. Through images of darkness and light again, Anne Brontë expresses the combination of both positive and negative aspects in that very physicality. Passion can both inspire and delude: "the hovering cloud cast over me by my aunt's views ... was lost in the bright effulgence of my own hopes and the too delightful consciousness of requited love" (173).

Offering ample symbolic indication that the relationship is doomed, Brontë also presents linked clues to the reason for its failure through iteration of the angel image. When Huntingdon addresses Helen as "angel" and "treasure," he is clearly not speaking to an equal; Helen, the stereotyped "saint," will be as fettered as if she were molded in plaster, unable to rise beyond the figurative kneeling position, trapped, emmarbled like the telling little busts that, in *Agnes Grey*, mark out Rosalie Ashby's sadly limited world (175). Clearly, Helen's fate is to be kept under his "roof" as an object, expected to display only those qualities of "sweet, attractive goodness" as serve to please the onlooker on a purely superficial level (174). As the angel motif is developed, it takes on the resonance of other image clusters associated with stereotypes of women as submissive servants and mysterious, stony-hearted priestess figures: the connected images that represent both the centrality and subjection of women are those of hearth and home, conjoined with the rock or stone images that serve as indications of Helen's emotional state.

To say that Helen's "angel" is countered by Huntingdon's "devil" would suggest a facile dichotomy, although Anne Brontë clearly demonstrates the satanic features of his character with unerring precision. As the disturbing details of Helen's diary unfold, Huntingdon's demonic tendencies emerge mainly in his ability to manipulate and undermine his wife. Helen's question to him, "And am *I* above all human sympathies?" is another ironic pointer to his inhuman treatment of her, for although he mockingly places her above her "earthly lord" in a "saintly" position for being "too religious," he actually treats her as one who is beneath his sympathies (205). Helen's query also emphasizes the imbalance inherent in elevating anyone (as Huntingdon attempts to do in word only) "towards that saintly condition" (205) which was reserved for women in the enforced role of "my household deity" (269)—a deeply ironic title bespeaking both ownership of the woman as venerated object and denial of her essential humanity, as in Coventry Patmore's *Angel in the House*.[14] Arthur's exalting epithets are, ironically, a means of dehumanizing Helen; when she is reduced to the saintly object, it becomes apparent that those "human sympathies" she invokes have been cleverly manipulated. Later identified by Jung as an aspect of the archetypal *anima*, this paradoxical splitting of the female figure into something at once divine and threatening reflects primitive man's ambivalence towards the monstrous power of the creating (and uncreating) universe. Similarly evoking the primitive consciousness of one who both needs and fears his wife's powerful female presence, Anne Brontë's representation of the unhealthy twist in the relationship between Helen and her psychologically destructive husband is particularly penetrating. This characterization of Huntingdon through word and deed shows him as a dangerously unbalanced figure who can only see women as types, fragments of the whole. His justification of infidelity is supported by the dubious reasoning that his mistress is, he assures Helen, "mere dust and ashes in comparison with you," and a "daughter of Earth," while his wife is "an angel of heaven" (237). The logic behind this statement is one of entrapment: the abuser's reductive language of extremes separates Helen from common humanity, effectively isolating her, and locking her into the household angel role as titular wife and housekeeper.

Seen through Huntingdon's warped mind, the angel epithet later takes on another twist. With the realization that death is near, he conjures up a bitterly cynical picture of Helen as "my immaculate angel" (his diseased construct) looking "complacently on" as he burns in hell. In the fearful anger of a moral coward, feeling powerless and guilty after his abusive control over her, he transfers his terror at the thought of eternal torment into a mocking manipulation of the indomitable Helen's virtue. In the ultimate powerlessness of death, he presumes that the powerful goodness of his former victim will be turned against him. Just as she is morally distanced from him in life, he wryly imagines her (like Lazarus to the rich man) frustratingly inaccessible to him in death as a vengeful angel who "would not so much as dip the tip of [her] finger in water to cool [his] tongue" (449). Helen's reply, with its biblical allusion to the separation between heaven and hell ("the great gulf over which I cannot pass") signifies the discrepancy between her consciousness and his, suggesting also another allegory of the difference between the new age and the old. Their personal differences correspond to what Juliet McMaster calls "the difference between Regency and Victorian mores," and she points out that generally Anne Brontë "uses the standard Victorian commentary on the excesses of the previous generation as a paradigm for the relationship between the sexes."[15]

That there is indeed a "great gulf" between Helen and her unregenerate husband is amply demonstrated by the novel's antithetical imagery, but, as Ewbank indicates, the contrast between Huntingdon's fear of damnation and Helen's assurance of salvation is a major concern for Anne Brontë, who questions "the horror of a situation without consolation," as emphatically here as in her poem "A Word to the Elect."[16] Her anti-Calvinist poem contains images that parallel the image patterns in *The Tenant*:

> You may rejoice to think *yourselves* secure;
> You may be grateful for the gift divine—
> That grace unsought, which made your black hearts pure,
> And fits your earth-born souls in Heaven to shine.   (*Poems* 89)

Explored at some length in the "glorious thought" of Helen's discussion with her aunt (178), Anne Brontë's argument in the poem expresses her belief that the hope of salvation for all gives light and life, as does true faith in a caring God who has designed egalitarian order and balance within the universe.

The chapter on Huntingdon's death ("The Rain Descended") indicates that Helen is not only released from her limited role as dutiful, ministering angel, but also given an opportunity to re-enter the waters of life and reclaim her personhood; this parting is the penultimate step in her realization of her whole self. No longer constrained by duty to remain in a marriage which is itself moribund, she is finally released from a situation which is aptly symbolized by "the darkened room where the sick man lay" (434). Gilbert's later allusion to "that incessant and deleterious confinement beside a living corpse" (457) describes a spiritual and emotional entombment which has now ended. Anne Brontë makes it clear that no matter how humanely concerned with his fate Helen might be, as long as Huntingdon lives, she cannot lead a completely fulfilling life—"still, while he lived, she *must* be miserable" (447)—suggesting that Helen's emotional entrapment is related to his continual manipulation of her maternal Christian feelings.

The interminable strife of Helen's marriage is given spiritual and emotional veracity by repeated use of this image scheme that sets demonic darkness against angelic light. An identical series of images appears in another context, where Brontë describes Helen's experience of being shadowed and then cornered by her would-be seducer, Walter Hargrave. The undercurrent of schism and confrontation lends further scope to Brontë's study of Helen's beleaguered psyche as she traces the tortuous passage of her relationship with Hargrave. Hargrave exhibits a persuasive attitude reminiscent of Milton's Satan, whose "fawning" flattery and "fraudulent temptation"[17] parallel the "insinuating friendship" (251) that Hargrave is so anxious to push upon Helen. In one of their earlier encounters, Hargrave is shown in an instructively symbolic position as the potential barrier to any remaining light in Helen's existence:

> The time that I met him alone was on a bright but not oppressively hot day in the beginning of July: I had taken little Arthur into the wood that skirts the park, and there seated him on the moss-cushioned roots of an old oak; and, having gathered a handful of bluebells and wild roses, I was kneeling before him . . . (251)

Into this picture of innocence, light and life, Hargrave is introduced as a sinister force: "a shadow suddenly eclipsed the little space of sunshine on the grass before us; and, looking up, I beheld Walter Hargrave standing and gazing upon us" (252). In the scenes of attempted seduction that follow, Anne Brontë uses the antithetical angel-devil motif to show how the fallen Hargrave attempts to manipulate Helen, the unfallen angel, through flattery and "bold yet artful eloquence" (329).

In its appeal to Helen's "super-human purity" and "perfections" (294), Hargrave's argument is a twisted reversal of the actual situation as he offers her the chance to "save" him sexually, citing her God-given ability to raise "a devoted heart from purgatorial torments to a state of heavenly bliss" (317). Helen, however, is intelligent enough to read the true meaning of his words, never losing sight of the reality that any liaison with him would have the reverse effect of bringing her down to a level of "purgatorial torment." Displaying the tawdry underside of a *carpe diem* motif that splits woman into manageable parts, Hargrave concludes that Helen is "my angel — my divinity!" and also that she is "only half a woman . . . half human, half angelic" (332), ending with a plea to her angelic potential to "save" him (by capitulating). Hargrave's deliberately misleading words, setting Helen apart (and up) only to knock her down, enact the cheap verbal tricks of a would-be seducer appealing to a lonely woman's physical and emotional vulnerability.

Helen's refusal of Hargrave's advances is accompanied by images of darkness and desolation. He attempts emotional blackmail through the rhetoric of urgent need and wasted potential: "my youth is wasting away:

my prospects are darkened; my life is a desolate blank" (335). His verbal *coup de grâce*, though, is an instructive parody of the argument used by Satan in *Paradise Lost*. Hargrave argues for Helen's compromising of her principles on the grounds that passion is among "the most godlike impulses of our nature" (335). Just as the serpent promises Eve "and ye shall be as Gods"[18] if she will eat the fruit, so Hargrave contends with "powerful sophistries" (336) that Helen is empowered to "raise" them both into a blessed state if she will capitulate: "You have it in your power to raise two human beings from a state of actual suffering to such unspeakable beatitude as only generous, noble self-forgetting love can give" (335). In this gripping dialogue, Anne Brontë's wry verbal acuity shows reversed meanings which emphasize the psychological truth behind the tempter's false rhetoric. Helen intuitively grasps that Hargrave's presentation of "power" to her actually signifies a loss of her power; rather than being raised she will be lowered. And, far from the "unspeakable beatitude" found through "noble self-forgetting love," what he offers is closer to unspeakable anguish in the wake of ignoble lust.

Throughout Hargrave's many attempts at seduction, Anne Brontë examines the shifting range of meaning behind the angelic symbol of purity (the angel in the house) which a male hegemony would use to subjugate and control women. When Hargrave's approaches have run the gamut of uses for the word "angel," from servile flattery to the quasi-religious fervor of emotional blackmail, he resorts to the notion of their co-equal sanctity, which here sounds distinctly sacrilegious:

> "You have no reason now: you are flying in the face of heaven's decrees. God has designed me to be your comfort and protector—I feel it—I know it as certainly as if a voice from heaven declared 'Ye twain shall be one flesh' and you spurn me from you—" (361)

The word picture here is an amalgam of metaphorical reference to good and evil, power and powerlessness, reputation and infamy; each facet of the picture is allusively interlinked through social and biblical references to marriage, its bogus religious authority emphasizing the psychological bombardment of this isolated woman who can only more acutely feel the lack of a marriage made in heaven upon hearing her seducer's travesty of wedding vows. As Hargrave glances at the window, a "gleam of malicious triumph [lights] up his countenance," and then Helen looks over her shoulder to see "a shadow just retiring round the corner" (361). The "gleam" of negative energy and the ominous archetypal symbol of the "shadow" signal Helen's precarious position.

Rapidly following this telling exchange, as Hargrave rushes to catch his quarry, his ironic description of Grimsby (the grim "shadow" behind the corner) neatly sums up the threat which he himself poses: "He has no love for you, Mrs. Huntingdon—no reverence for your sex—no belief in virtue—no admiration for its image" (361-62). Helen's retort that this coercion is an "insult" draws a desperate (but brief) repetition of the worshipping stance: "I do not insult you . . . I worship you. You are my angel—my divinity! I lay my powers at your feet—and you must and shall accept them!" (362). Alternating tersely declarative with sharply imperative statements, the forceful language combines here with angel imagery to work as ironic signifiers in repeated references to a feigned submission which is actually the mask of dominance. With the closing contradiction of the submissive "lay my powers at your feet" and the imperatives "must and shall," the point is made that it is but a short step from such bogus veneration to subjugation. When all the maneuvers have failed, Hargrave's bitter summary of Helen's character contains in essence what the novelist has been illustrating all along. Stripped of its "bitter emphasis," Hargrave's statement, "you are the most cold-hearted, unnatural, ungrateful woman," unintentionally reveals the underlying truth that he is not (nor was he ever) dealing with an "angel" but with a warm-blooded, natural, intelligent woman, albeit a woman who has every reason to be "ungrateful" (362).

This kind of literary cross-referencing, using the angel-devil and heaven-hell motifs with their allusion to the Fall and divine retribution, serves to create an atmosphere of deeply entrenched hostility and spiritual schism. As the narrative unfolds, an omnipresent pull between good and evil is revealed, and the diary entries show that the beleaguered protagonist must find sanctuary from destructive forces in order to survive. In this hostile environment, the most obvious place of sanctuary is not always the best. After one of Hargrave's early advances, Helen retreats "within the sanctum" of her home, a place where, ironically, any vestige of sanctuary is seriously threatened (253). But in *The Tenant*, even more than in *Agnes Grey*, the home and its hearth are a particular focus for the clash of values, the thematic oppositions—spirit against flesh, liberty against oppression—which dominate the entire novel. More than once, either Helen or Gilbert (even Huntingdon early in the marriage) is pictured leaning on the chimney breast, returning for sustenance, it would seem, to the heart of the home, the core of old values and old structures, to find solutions to seemingly impossible contradictions. But rather than providing solutions, the fireside settings seem to reflect societal and psychological problems. When Helen, for example, seeks solace at the hearth in the library during Huntingdon's courtship, she receives scant comfort from the "faint red glow of the neglected fire" (164), an emblem that portends the faintness of his love for her and the neglect she suffers. As a woman (and, in the traditional male view, an embodiment of the household deity), Helen is the keeper of the hearth: it symbolizes her traditional role and her traditional strengths, such as compassion, nurturing, fortitude and patience. But, just as the most obvious refuge is not always best, in *The Tenant* the hearth image is fraught with conflicting meanings, for Helen's traditional role is rewritten when she moves away from her "proper" place as submissive domestic hearthkeeper and lives a rigorously independent life, much to the dismay of established local residents. While the warmth of the blazing fire at Linden Car encompasses all the complacently tidy familial values of the Markhams, the firesides at Grass-dale and Wildfell Hall reflect stages in their proprietor's departure from those standards. The hearth is therefore an ambiguous symbol in the novel.

The closely-knit, but comparatively rigid structures of the Markham household are indicated in the way the fireside image is articulated. For example, although there is warmth in Gilbert's house, the traditional warmth evinced by his mother's "blazing fire" cools perceptibly when an unconventional stranger enters the cosy family circle. In contrast to the welcoming reception extended to all the local worthies by the Markhams, both mother and daughter express deeply ingrained suspicion towards anything or anyone remotely untraditional, especially when the unrepentant iconoclast is a single woman. When Gilbert, questioning his patrimony, arrives home after working on the farm "one cold, damp, cloudy evening" (7), the warm glow of the fire—significantly kept under the doting matriarchal eye of his mother—cheers him and offers a socially constructed "haven of bliss" (8). Anne Brontë carefully sketches in the details of the room where tea is served as Mrs. Markham, "that honoured lady," who has denied her vision of Gilbert's "higher aims" by complying with her husband's deathbed exhortation, sits and knits:

> She had swept the hearth, and made a bright blazing fire for our reception; the servant had just brought in the tea-tray; and Rose was producing the sugar basin and tea caddy, from the cupboard in the black, oak sideboard, that shone like polished ebony, in the cheerful parlour twilight. (8)

Everything in this setting—a life arranged in "the good old way" by Gilbert's father whose final entreaty has kept them on the "paternal acres" (7)—is very neatly ordered: there is a place for everyone and all the family members know their place. The setting's pointed shaping by the patriarchal dictum that opens the chapter ("to continue in the good old way, to follow his steps and those of his father before him") inscribes an ironic twist into the "cheerful parlour" where, despite the warm compliance of its traditional female occupants, Helen is predictably judged and found wanting by local society because she clearly does not easily fit into place. The mother's judgment that Helen betrays "a lamentable ignorance on certain points" is based partly on her lack of culinary skill ("all the little niceties of cookery, and such things that every lady ought to be familiar with" [12]), and partly on her determination to take the unprecedented step of discouraging her small son from drinking alcohol (against the dubious expression of popular conservative values, she refuses to make "a man . . . of him" [27]). Rose Markham, who fits so neatly into the fireside picture when "producing the sugar-basin and tea-caddy," pronounces her inability to place Helen in the conventional scheme of things: "I don't know what to make of her, at all" (44). And Mrs. Markham is similarly nonplussed when she addresses the party of local notables gathered in her firelit parlour at Linden-Car, with a dismissive "we don't know what to make of her" (36). When her hidebound guests learn of the "mistaken ideas and conduct" of that "very singular lady," even the vicar, a satirical embodiment of the hypocritical grotesque, is moved to outright condemnation: "criminal, I should say—criminal" (38). From the outset, then, Brontë shows that a single woman of such independent, almost anti-social, persuasions is not to be admitted easily into the inner circle of fireside friends.

Whereas the interior of Linden-Car is conventional and comfortable (for those who "belong" there), the inside of Wildfell Hall provides an austere contrast in keeping with the unconventional, problematic circumstances of its inhabitants. This image of the ruined Hall, a relic of the Virgin Queen's age when women were richly celebrated in poetical outpourings that blazoned the feminine principle embodied in a powerful, solitary monarch, adds emphasis to the fate of its marginalized tenant. Its surroundings, as Gilbert relates, are analogous to Helen's doughty inner self, for the hall stands defiantly on the "wildest and loftiest eminence in our neighbourhood," where only the toughest of plants survive the "war of wind and weather":

> Near the top of this hill, about two miles from Linden-Car, stood Wildfell Hall, a superannuated mansion of the Elizabethan era, built of dark grey stone,—venerable and picturesque to look at, but, doubtless, cold and gloomy enough to inhabit, with its thick stone mullions and little latticed panes, its time-eaten air-holes, and its too lonely, too unsheltered situation,—only shielded from

the war of wind and weather by a group of Scotch firs, themselves half blighted with storms and looking as stern and gloomy as the Hall itself. (18-19)

Although parodic undertones of *Wuthering Heights* emerge quite clearly from this description, they do so in a way that registers Anne Brontë's radical determination to re-write other Romantic models. While Helen is like the characters from the Heights in her unconventionality, the tenant of this windlashed outpost is a social pioneer who independently sets out to restructure her own social order, and, unlike the inhabitants of the Heights, she achieves this primarily through rationality rather than passion. She is clearly an argument for the combination of intelligent emotion with reason. The description of the Hall which provides Helen refuge is also a metaphor for the abused woman within, "unsheltered" and "too lonely," who has seen the glory of earlier days and may rightly appear "stern and gloomy" but, as the narrative demonstrates, can stand fast against the blighting storms of opposition and retain a "venerable" integrity.

The cold isolation in which Helen must live is reinforced by the chill interior of her living quarters with their pointedly "empty grate" (42). Unlike her distant neighbors at Linden-Car, Helen denies herself the warmth of a blazing fire, with its implications of chauvinistic community and female compliance. After her official ostracism by the patriarchy, personified in the reverend Michael Millward, Helen is visited by an outraged and fiercely protective Gilbert. She is revealed through a window "slowly pacing up and down her lonely room" (97), which Gilbert insists is "gloomy" for the want of a fire. If Helen's external situation is "dismal" (97), we are keenly aware that it reflects her inner discomfort. She has, of course, chosen to step out of the comfortable tradition of wifeliness and eschews all urgings to revert to a set mode of behavior that she can well do without. "But *we always* have a fire in the evenings—if we can bear it," insists Gilbert, re-affirming the established order of his home, whereas Helen is aware that she is destined to depart from the comfortable norm:

> "Me comfortable!" repeated she, with a bitter laugh, as if there were something amusingly absurd in the idea. "It suits me better as it is," she added in a tone of mournful resignation. (98)

Her resigned aside that this frigid state of affairs suits her suggests that she must wear her comfortless isolation as an outward sign of her separate identity.

Gilbert, however, would prefer to change the situation, and (within the extended range of the hearth symbol) his need to take charge and make a fire clearly demonstrates that it is not just an interest in Helen's comfort which prompts his "fancy for a fire" (98). Conflated in this fireside image is the lure of domesticity, the wish to construct a cosy refuge from external social pressures and a desire for possession of the loved one. It also represents the fire of growing sexual response and, as the abused wife must anticipate, the violent possibility of entrapment and submission:

> In a little while we both relapsed into silence, and continued for several minutes gazing abstractedly into the fire—she intent upon her own sad thoughts, and I reflecting how delightful it would be to be seated thus beside her with no other presence to restrain our intercourse . . . (98-99)

Gilbert's reverie as he imagines their potential togetherness combines with the fire image here to emphasize the lack of light or warmth, in short, the absence of "delightful" social intercourse in Helen's life. The effect is similar to the way the fire burning in the grate signifies the lack of family harmony in Anne Brontë's poem "Monday Night May 11th 1846." There, despite the redly burning fire, "still the hearth is desolate" (*Poems* 129), just as it is in the scene with Helen and Gilbert.

The fire, then, sums up all the heated intensity of feeling which Helen must avoid, the life force which she must deny herself because it is inextricably caught up in a destructive status quo. A comment by Terry Eagleton on Charlotte Brontë's novels is particularly relevant here, because it applies equally well to the process at hand, in which we see Anne's treatment of thematic concerns through varying and recurrent image clusters. Charlotte's novels, Eagleton says, "dramatise a conflict between 'morality' and 'society' but the two sets of values are subtly intertwined, so that to live well involves both eagerly embracing the world and firmly fending it off."[19] It seems to me that this is also the kind of self-division generated by Helen's carefully authenticated marginal position. Her social and emotional self (signified above in the hearth) cannot be realized until her life has been stripped of all its social trappings, reevaluated (which requires "fending off" the world), and then reconstituted in a whole and healthy "embracing" of the world which gestures beyond the limits of a purely moral self. In the words of Anne Brontë's poem to the Calvinists (which Ewbank has identified as an important basis of the "spiritual dimension" permeating *The Tenant*),[20] "before their dross is purged away" (*Poems* 90), neither Helen nor Huntingdon can move on to the next step. The allusion is generally taken to apply to the unrepentant sinner (such as Huntingdon), but it could similarly be applied to Helen, who recognizes the need to cleanse herself of sin.[21]

As in *Agnes Grey*, the image of the fireside performs a double function: it serves to illustrate the traditional nexus of family life, and it also reminds the reader that physical warmth is incomplete without emotional warmth and integrity. The poetic realization of a dissociated emotional state in "Monday Night May 11th 1846" also reveals the kind of emptiness that both Gilbert and Helen experience in the absence of love. This feeling of alienation is apparent in a series of comparable fireside settings, from Grass-dale to Staningly, illustrating at the same time a changing dynamic of gender relations. The emotional stance of the characters is figuratively displayed by their bodily stance in relation to the hearth. During his penultimate encounter with Helen at Wildfell Hall, before she gives him the vindicating diary (Chapter 15), Gilbert stands firmly with his back to the fire-place in an attitude of confrontation; as he surveys an unflinchingly righteous Helen, he expresses an exultant sense of power which is reminiscent of that enjoyed by Huntingdon, although for quite contrasting reasons: "'I can crush that bold spirit,' thought I. But while I secretly exulted in my power, I felt disposed to dally with my victim like a cat" (123). Filled with the briefly sociopathic anger of imagined betrayal, Gilbert at this point is turning his back on hearth and heart, turning away from their potential union and rejecting any domestic bliss that Helen might stand for; he is turning against the feminine principle because it now threatens his integrity, Helen having cruelly betrayed him (or so he mistakenly believes) by secretly joining with his rival, Frederick Lawrence. Helen, by comparison, "leant against one end of the chimneypiece, opposite that near which I was standing, with her chin resting on her closed hand" (124). Her body registers the wearying stress of alienation, while her eyes speak of the "restless excitement" (124) that betrays both her intellectual and her passionate self.

Since chapter headings are important structural pointers throughout Anne Brontë's novels, it is significant that this description of Helen's physical stance is found in the "Encounter" chapter (suggesting the meeting of equals), whereas Arthur Huntingdon's similarly ambiguous pose by the hearth appears in the later chapter entitled "First Quarrel." Huntingdon is shown in "an attitude of undisguised dejection, leaning against the chimney-piece with his forehead sunk upon his arm" (215). As in the earlier chapter, the emphasis falls on the eyes which belie a dejected stance, here contrived to incline towards a forgiving, compassionate core, the heart of the home, symbolized by the hearth upon which he leans so demonstratively.

Huntingdon's eyes, however, tell a contradictory story, revealing that this entire display of penitence and submission is feigned in order to manipulate Helen. When Helen asks if he is penitent, his reaction tells the whole story: "'Heart-broken!' he answered, with a rueful countenance—yet with a merry smile just lurking within his eyes and about the corners of his mouth" (216). Once the manipulative tactics (which gain emphasis by comparison with Helen's genuine anguish in the previous fireside setting) pay their expected dividend of Helen's sympathetic response, his stance immediately changes to one of arrant superiority, noticeably similar to Gilbert's confrontational attitude hard by the hearth in Wildfell Hall: "He now turned round and stood facing me, with his back to the fire" (216). As Huntingdon gains the upper hand, he does exactly what Gilbert is tempted to do in response to Helen's supposed duplicity; he reduces his "victim" to the level of plaything and, standing with his back to the fire, challenges her, "Come then, Helen, are you going to be a good girl?" (216). In direct contrast to Gilbert, Huntingdon betrays motives colored by the urge to control rather than to love, and Helen's response to her husband's insincerity indicates that she is aware of this: "This sounded rather too arrogant, and the smile that accompanied it did not please me" (216).

These fireside images and scenes reverberate throughout the novel, often working ironically—given the usual associations of fireside warmth —to reveal the gulfs in human relations. When, for example, Helen and Gilbert finally discuss "the matter of eternal separation" (405) towards the end of the novel, the rent in Helen's composure is keenly drawn, both in external gesture and in the symbolism of the empty fireplace. While Helen is a composite of antagonistic forces in her appearance ("the constriction of her brow, the tight compression of her lips, and wringing of her hands"), the repeatedly mentioned empty fireplace economically signifies that, although torn by "a violent conflict between reason and passion . . . silently passing within her," her choice is made and reason has won (404-405). Gilbert's gesture, leaning his head against a cold chimney breast in an echo of Huntingdon's earlier stance, appeals to a domestic deity which has no place in their lives: "'End here!' echoed I; and approaching the high, carved chimney-piece, I leant my hand against its heavy mouldings, and dropped my forehead upon it in silent, sullen despondency" (405). The parallels with that earlier marital fireplace provide a reference point by which to measure the progress of Brontë's protagonist; they also emphasize the contrast between Gilbert's heartfelt depth of feeling and Huntingdon's crass superficiality. By this stage, Helen has learned to operate as an autonomous being, her determination to reconcile passion with reason summed up in the reiterated description of her "desperate calmness" (409). No longer subservient or dependent in any way, she now can demand from Gilbert an equal share of responsibility in their relationship. In knowing the fullness of a liberated self, she also knows the meaning of egalitarian co-existence, and can insist that Gilbert be "a true friend," shoulder his "own part in the struggle of right against passion," and not "leave all the burden to me" (406). This last scene by the cold hearth, then, signifies a figurative dampening of their relationship's flame by Helen's necessarily cool rationality, a kind of emotional hiatus before the love between Helen and Gilbert can be regenerated in a stronger form.

Probably the most powerful use of the hearth image is seen when the fire is introduced as an agent of violation in Helen's own inner sanctum —the library, a figure for the mind. Helen specifically identifies the library as a safe place where she can escape abuse: "Since Lord Lowborough's departure I had regarded the library as entirely my own, a secure retreat at all hours of the day" (357). Huntingdon not only invades that inner sanctum, he also appropriates the light from the fire (her own creative, nurturing fire) in order to read her diary, even after she has attempted to protect her privacy by extinguishing the candles. Next, in an ultimate violation of her private self, he burns all her painting equipment, her sole remaining means of independent expression. This symbolic burning of Helen's creativity and identity stresses the criminal trick which is played on the obedient wife who abides by the social code, only to discover that this very code can be the agent of her destruction. At this climactic point, the fire which consumes her artistic endeavors and her hopes of freedom points to the destruction of the marriage itself. Helen has been true to her calling, having kept the household flame burning at great personal cost, only to have it used against her. Her husband derives considerable pleasure in taunting her with her own decent sobriety and reminding her that she is trapped, while he is free to give his energetic concern to a demi-mondaine and deride the "rigid severity" of a "gloomy . . . ascetic" wife who stands by him (387). While Huntingdon frets over his "dear Annabella," Helen is scorned:

> everything I did was wrong; I was cold-hearted, hard, insensate; my sour pale face was perfectly repulsive; my voice made him shudder; he knew not how he could live through the winter with me; I should kill him by inches. Again I proposed a separation, but it would not do: he was not going to be the talk of the neighbourhood . . . no; he must contrive to bear with me. (322)

As a social document, this narrative record of mental abuse is extraordinarily powerful. Such keenly observed psychological detail in the flat delivery of this list of accusations, punctuated by withering pejoratives ("wrong," "hard," "insensate," "repulsive"), represents depression in all its leaden heaviness. Delivered in Huntingdon's cruel voice, but focalized in Helen's consciousness *qua* trapped object, the narrative here gives a probing enactment of severe mental abuse from the victim's point of view. The acuteness of Brontë's implied political analysis of entrenched attitudes is enhanced by the fireside setting, which in this context conveys a sardonic comment on society's double standards and endorsement of destructive power relations.

Thus trapped in the irreconcilable spaces of abuser and victim, Helen and Huntingdon live in two alien worlds of "Dual Solitude," heralded by the chapter heading, which underlines the tension between the two characters in this abusive situation. Helen's entrapment in this loveless, deadening marriage is pointed in the allusions to death and imprisonment, to her affectionate feelings having been "wholly crushed and withered away" (323), and to the "bondage" of their union (325). Ironically, while Huntingdon twists her sombre integrity into reasons why she is an unsuitable parent, it is only the close communion with her son (as both parent and teacher) and her painting which keep Helen herself from being "killed by inches" (322). Nevertheless, the psychic devastation that results when these creative avenues of escape are blocked results in a state evocative of death. Huntingdon's destruction of her worktools is an *avant la lettre* portrayal of psychotic transference: not only does he see his own "cold-hearted" repulsiveness in his wife, but he is also attempting to force his own mindlessness upon her, to quench her creative spirit forever and make her as he is. Helen's resulting death-like torpor is another accurately observed psychological state, entirely fitting to the overwhelming stress suffered by women at the hands of such abusers. Helen recalls her utterly drained energy in a series of adjectives that express loss as "less": "I did not attempt to follow him, but remained seated in the arm-chair, speechless, tearless, and almost motionless" (370).

A veritably tactile impression of this kind of emotional wasting is conveyed throughout *The Tenant* in a series of images of petrifaction. If the hearth imagery is an objective correlative for the social and emotional status of the characters, then imagery of hardness and softness operates along similar lines to further define emotional and social interactions (or expectations). Anne Brontë is manifestly aware of the social requirements of womanhood, and she searchingly subjects the soft, submissive "angel" type to the radical scrutiny of her fundamentally egalitarian viewpoint.[22] Early in the novel, for example, Helen takes part in a discussion on educational discrimination between boys and girls, referring deprecatingly to the practice of treating a girl "tenderly and delicately . . . like a hot house plant—taught to cling to others for direction or support and guarded as much as possible from the very knowledge of evil" (30). The voice of this intelligent iconoclast no doubt echoes Brontë's own in insisting that autonomy gives strength and self-reliance:

> I would not send a poor girl into the world, unarmed against foes, and ignorant of the snares that beset her path; nor would I watch and guard her, till, deprived of self-respect and self-reliance, she lost the power or the will to watch and guard herself. (30)

Brontë's exploration of the ambiguities contained in that social prerequisite of "softness" (for women at least) enlarges on the distinction between "wholesome truth" and "soft nonsense" made in the Preface to *The Tenant*. Her social analysis in the novel is imbued with the balanced conviction (also expressed in her preface) that what is appropriate for a man should be equally appropriate for a woman.[23] In the course of her narrative, suggestive iteration of specifically related images prompts the reader to consider the tensions between public and private constructions of the self: what may be publicly construed as "hardness" (Mr. Millward's verdict on a shockingly unconventional Helen is an emphatic "'Hardened, I fear—hardened!'" [95]), here signifying the refusal to conform to repressive norms, is distinct from the private experience of "hardness" (through physical suffering, brutality, harsh experience), which can lead either to growth or to spiritual constriction. Anne Brontë's grasp of this underlying psychological variance is set out in the suggestive thought-lines of her connected image schemes.

Throughout *The Tenant* she remains true to her credo that hardship produces character, and through the repeated juxtapositions of contrasting tactile images, her rhetoric demonstrates that softness is not a sign of excellence in woman. All too often, the softness so much a part of the Victorian picture of womanhood is allied to dishonesty or deceit, of the kind that Coventry Patmore lauds with fervently sadomasochistic tones in *Angel in the House*. He writes about feminine guiles in the canto ominously titled "The Koh-i-Noor," where he equates this glittering imago of a woman with creatures variously sweet and cunning, but creatures nonetheless:

> And, evermore, for either's sake,
> To the sweet folly of the dove,
> She joins the cunning of the snake,
> To rivet and exalt his love.[24]

But while Patmore connects the Koh-i-Noor diamond with woman as commodity in the market of sexual exchange, chillingly claiming that "A woman like the Koh-i-Noor, / Mounts to the price that's put on her,"[25] Anne Brontë deploys rock and stone imagery to urge a far more solidly honest, healthy rationality in human relations. By conflating a more instructive combination of meanings within her stone imagery, she redefines the reductive symbolism traditionally applied to women to suggest that the hardness of experience and the independent strength of maturity are interlocked.

Through significantly juxtaposed images of hardness and softness at the beginning of the novel, Helen's features are compared with those of Eliza Millward. While Helen's lips are "a little too firmly compressed and had something about them that betokened, I thought, no very soft or amiable temper" (13), Eliza's features are distinguished by her eyes ("diabolically-wicked, or irresistably bewitching—often both") and her voice, which is tellingly childlike:

> gentle and childish, her tread light and soft as that of a cat;—but her manners more frequently resembled those of a pretty, playful kitten, that is now pert and roguish, now timid and demure, according to its own sweet will. (15)

Gilbert's observations on the two women reflect his original preferences. Huntingdon's description of Helen, however, depicts a fierce "hard" adversary through images of harshly flashing eyes ("you stand there with your white face and flashing eyes, looking at me like a very tigress" [211]), while Gilbert writes that her eyes are "full of soul" (62). The contrast between Helen, the complex, independent woman, and Eliza, the charming, compliant girl, is thus drawn by the use of contrasting imagery. The superiority of a woman like Helen, who withdraws from all hints of flirtation is clear: a mere smile from Gilbert initially brings forth her "proud, chilly look" and "a look of repellent scorn" (22). Eliza, on the other hand, is the epitome of coquettishness as she flirts with Gilbert by the contrivance of "overwhelming her sister's pet [cat] with a shower of kisses," and giving Gilbert "one of her softest smiles and most bewitching glances" (23). Although Gilbert first thinks Helen "too hard, too sharp, too bitter for my taste," it is not long before the "soft, yet unrelenting sway" (49) of Eliza begins to pall and Gilbert finds her "rather frivolous, and even a little insipid, compared with the more mature and earnest

Mrs. Graham" (49). Eliza's "mild, reproachful sadness" and "gentle melancholy" (67) are "soft" veneers that cover an unpleasant harshness and malice; Gilbert's final perception of her character is negative—he calls her "the little demon" (426).

This perceptual *volte face*, as Gilbert places the women in his life more accurately according to their depth of character, also occurs in his reading of Helen, as he recognizes that what appears to the undiscerning as "hardness" in her is actually integrity, uncommon intelligence, and strength of character which has been forged largely through adversity. This theme is evoked directly in Helen's ironic oak tree analogy, which she amusingly utters with some self-deprecation:

> Such experience, to him (to use a trite simile), will be like the storm to the oak, which, though it may scatter the leaves, and snap the smaller branches, serves but to rivet the roots, and to harden and condence [*sic*] the fibres of the tree. (30)

The apparent contradiction here is that Helen is arguing against the kind of exposure to sordid reality which has strengthened her. In the case of her son, on whose behalf she argues against "practical acquaintance with forbidden things" (30), her greatest concern is that seeing life in all its sick depravity (the life lived by his lecherous, drunken father) should not corrupt him.

This fear of corruption is explored in *The Tenant* (as earlier in *Agnes Grey*) through the imagery of petrifaction. In deep despair at the unrelieved baseness of her husband's ways, Helen makes an anguished declaration that her heart has turned to stone: "I think the petrifaction is so completely effected at last, that nothing can melt me again" (325). Her bitter self-examination echoes Agnes Grey's alienated despair: "Already I seemed to feel my intellect deteriorating, my heart petrifying, my soul contracting" (*Agnes Grey* 103). In Agnes's distress at the worldly exploitation that surrounds her, she fears, as Ewbank explains, that "this kind of life is actually contaminating her."[26] Helen's words express a similar fear: "hence I must be, and I am debased, contaminated by the union both in my own eyes and in the actual truth" (263).

At some deeper level of awareness, Helen admits that her hardening is some necessary part of maturation. The petrifaction she laments in her emotional self is a self-defensive response to the destructive anguish of being psychologically beaten, a process she remarks upon with perceptive vehemence: "It is a hard, embittering thing to have one's kind feelings and good intentions cast back in one's teeth" (324). Through a psychologically adept crossover of meaning, Anne Brontë shows Helen appropriating the image originally suggested by her accusatory husband, for it is Huntingdon who first throws out the accusation that her heart has turned to stone:

> I believe he was much disappointed that I did not feel his offensive sayings more acutely, for when he had said anything particularly well calculated to hurt my feelings, he would stare me searchingly in the face, and then grumble against my "marble heart," or my "brutal insensibility." (323)

Doubly effective, in that it illustrates how Huntingdon has insinuated himself into her consciousness and destroyed her sense of self, this passage also demonstrates Helen's hardening as a direct result of her husband's brutality and indicates a mirroring of his own "brutal insensibility" in her repression. Here, the stone imagery thus makes a point about the futility of feminine "softness" in the face of overt (or even covert) sexual aggression. Nothing could be more removed from Patmore's morbid assertion that women love the "dear despot" and do so "for his mastering air": if Patmore's view accurately reflects Victorian mores, then Anne Brontë's study of marital tyranny radically departs from the mainstream on this point.[27] She is unequivocal in her portrayal of Huntingdon's despotism as morally repellent and emotionally ruinous:

> I was beginning to relent towards my wretched partner . . . and what was the result? No answering spark of kindness—no awakening penitence, but an unappeasable ill-humour and a spirit of tyrannous exaction that increased with indulgence, and a lurking gleam of self-complacent triumph, at every detection of relenting softness in my manner, that congealed me to marble again as often as it recurred. (325)

Rather than falling apart as she might be expected to do under such devastating circumstances, Helen is shown to remain firmly intact and later recognizes that her hardness is an essential part of her survival. The conclusion she reaches echoes Anne Brontë's perceptible bias towards fortitude and rationality as opposed to the airy-fairy "soft nonsense" (xxxvii) preached by those such as Patmore (and others closer to home). The figure of a battered but unbowed Helen exemplifies the toughening process and expresses the necessity of learned grit:

> And could I have imagined that I should have been able to endure it as calmly, and to repel their insults as firmly and as boldly as I had done? A hardness such as this, is taught by rough experience and despair alone. (365)

Clearly, then, Helen's "petrifaction" is a required withdrawal from the world. At the same time, her endurance allows her to stand up for herself and be strong in the face of a savagely abusive psychological onslaught. Helen's protective emotional "hardness" is, however, of an altogether different origin and nature from the brittle worldliness evinced by Mrs. Hargrave. Helen's terse assessment of Mrs. Hargrave's character is plain speaking at its best: "I don't like Mrs. Hargrave; she is a hard, pretensious [*sic*], worldly-minded woman" (231). Unlike Helen, whose "rough experience" toughens her outwardly while deepening her spiritual resolve to reconstruct a morally better life, Mrs. Hargrave embodies the hardness of spiritual paucity. Her heart is hardened in the biblical sense of one not capable of spirituality, and her consciousness is limited to the perception of material display and false power: "she is ever straining to keep up appearances, with that despicable pride that shuns the semblance of poverty as of a shameful crime" (231).

That women like Mrs. Hargrave and Helen are poles apart is firmly established in Anne Brontë's delineation of character through these antithetical images of hardness and softness: Helen learns inner strength from life in a way that is essentially alien to the Mrs. Hargraves of society. While Helen's "hardness" is a seasoned wholeness which will only permit the steadfastness of honesty and the unwavering magnanimity of egalitarian commitment, Mrs. Hargrave's "hardness" is a sign of psycho-social rigidity. Arguing for a kind of hard or solid autonomy in women rather than a mindlessly yielding softness, Brontë offers a brief synopsis of these contrasting characteristics through the unlikely mouthpiece of Hattersley. By means of a simple rock versus sand analogy, the bluffly-drawn Hattersley makes a case for the independent woman who is not "yielding," but stands firm (289). He initially compares his long-suffering, passive wife, Milicent (a model of angelic meekness), with the spirited, adamantine "creature" Annabella Lowborough (287). Since Annabella and the stables are mentioned in the same breath, one has the impression that Hattersley has in mind a fine brood mare (the "Black Bess" he admires) rather than a woman, particularly when he speaks of her as a "splendid creature" with "magnificent black eyes" and "a fine spirit of her own" (287). Having thus distinguished Annabella from his soft little wife, he goes on to make an important declaration about the need for a strong, unyielding spirit in marriage:

> And did you never, Milly, observe the sands on the seashore; how nice and smooth they look, and how soft and easy they feel to the foot? But if you plod along, for half an hour, over this soft, easy carpet—giving way at every step, yielding the more the harder you press,—you'll find it rather wearisome work, and be glad enough to come to a bit of good firm rock, that won't budge an

inch whether you stand, walk, or stamp upon it; and, though it be hard as the nether millstone, you'll find it the easier footing after all. (289)

Within this analogy, the strategically placed image of "good firm rock" which has the useful hardness of the millstone illustrates how Helen's pragmatic hardness must be read: not as the sign of a diminished spirit, but rather as an indication of her steadfastness and unshifting integrity. As such, it is the strong "footing" that forms a necessary stage in her developmental journey.

That Anne Brontë deliberately presents Helen as a pilgrim engaged in a journey of self-discovery, is amply attested by her repeated use of pathway and journey motifs throughout the novel. Indeed, as in *Agnes Grey*, the geography of the narrative can be mapped as criss-crossed by boundaries over which Helen must pass as she progresses. Chapter headings for the second volume read like a strategic escape plan: "Comparisons: Information Rejected," "Concealment," "Provocations," "A Scheme of Escape," "A Misadventure," "The Boundary Past," "The Retreat," "Startling Intelligence." Significantly, the first chapter of this volume, "Domestic Scenes," sets the position inside an enclosed space, while all the other titles point to careful planning and slow progress out of the domestic world. The last heading, "Fluctuations," suggests a freedom of movement which has taken Helen outside that restricted space.

Although Phyllis Bentley avers that Anne Brontë's cultural "vision was not wide," she goes on to affirm that her exterior settings are "described in words of considerable expressiveness and strength."[28] A good part of this expressive strength comes from the representation of the outdoor world in ways that suggest the natural order as an escape from social and psychological bondage. In *The Tenant* this escape takes on a multi-dimensional shape: one dimension is the literal narrative, as Helen passes down the road which leads her away from Grass-dale and her marriage; another is the metaphorical world of the imagination which liberates her inwardly as she roams the wild fells seeking artistic fulfilment and spiritual solace through her study of the landscape. Anne Brontë's well-documented love for Cowper's poetry supports the impression that she saw the same sense of comfort and delight in the outdoors. Suggesting through recurrent nature imagery the creating hand of a benevolent God in the beauty of the outdoors, she formulates a setting where divine communion is an ever-present actuality.[29]

Possibly the most memorable journey Helen makes through this divinely configured natural world, certainly the most crucial step she takes, is her flight from Grass-dale. As Helen flees, a scenic gathering of key images characterizes the momentous step and gives divine sanction to the fugitive woman in making it:

> What trembling joy it was when the little wicket closed behind us, as we issued from the park! Then, for one moment, I paused, to inhale one draught of that cool, bracing air, and venture one look back upon the house. All was dark and still; no light glimmered in the windows; no wreath of smoke obscured the stars that sparkled above it in the frosty sky. As I bade farewell for ever to that place, the scene of so much guilt and misery, I felt glad that I had not left it before, for now there was no doubt about the propriety of such a step—no shadow of remorse for him I left behind: there was nothing to disturb my joy but the fear of detection; and every step removed us farther from the chance of that. (394)

In this central passage images found throughout Anne Brontë's writings provide a clue to her method of linking the commonplace detail with the spiritual and emotional experience of her characters. The "wicket gate" (echoing the landscape of Bunyan's *Pilgrim's Progress*) and the "park" signify Helen's passage out of worldly corruption, away from both established social structures and captivity; the "cool, bracing air" she breathes as she looks back to the house signals a rebirth in the figurative "breath of life" she takes as she leaves domestic oppression and makes her way into the freedom of the open air; the darkness, enlivened by the stars sparkling in the frosty sky, evokes the dark depression caused by "so much guilt and misery" and the enlightened move towards liberty fired by celestial impulses.

The sky, often presented by Anne Brontë as a medium of communication with heaven, is another significant image that conveys the comforting message of divine benevolence for the fugitives in a starry night. With their twinkling energy, the stars suggest divine ciphers in an air of undefiled purity about the scene, where the lack of smoke implies that the house's contamination cannot touch this God-given message of hope. Based in Anne Brontë's outspoken concern with a doctrine of divine forgiveness, this metaphorical intimation of celestial acceptance or protection is a vital statement. Seen thus, within the philosophical framework of the narrative, the starlit sky demonstrates how it is only in the presence of this clear heavenly sanction that Helen can move on and take the liberating road ahead.

As well as the freedom of the outdoors, however, the scene shows a backward glance to the house at Grass-dale, with its dark windows and cold fireplace. Often in Anne Brontë's writing, windows symbolize both the imagination and the link between inner and outer worlds; they also represent a time-space continuum where both past and future coalesce. Here the blacked-out windows, signifying that no future remains for Helen in that lifeless place, also reveal the soulless and hopeless condition of the house's remaining occupants. Anne Brontë's poetic language reinforces the contrast between the house and the freedom beyond it. The crisp plosives in "stars that sparkled" counter the heavy vowels and halting rhythm of the phrase "the scene of so much guilt and misery" (394). Together, evocative language and imagery promise a new beginning with the conviction that Helen leaves her hell for good, a "prison and despair behind me" (395). Unlike Agnes Grey's cold autumn journey, which takes place at the same time of year, this one is full of joyful expectation, the positive energy of which colors the response to a countryside "all smiling—cheerfully, gloriously, smiling in the yellow lustre of those early beams" (395). The anthropomorphized "smiling" land is an allusion to God's nurturing love which echoes poems such as "Retirement," where Anne Brontë expresses the need to "Bask in the sunshine of the sky, / And be alone with God!" (*Poems* 77). The expressive language chosen to describe Helen's "retreat" from torment and the excited running together of short positive phrases create an impetuous musical rhythm, which rings with purposive energy:

> Oh, what delight it was to be thus seated aloft, rumbling along the broad, sunshiny road, with the fresh morning breeze in my face, surrounded by an unknown country all smiling—cheerfully, gloriously, smiling in the yellow lustre of those early beams,—with my darling child in my arms, almost as happy as myself and my faithful friend beside me; a prison and despair behind me, receding farther, farther back at every clatter of the horses' feet,—and liberty and hope before! I could hardly refrain from praising God aloud for my deliverance, or astonishing my fellow passengers by some surprising outburst of hilarity. (395)

Repetitions and assonance—"farther, farther"—recreate the open-mouthed wonder of triumphant release in this verbal enactment of liberation.

After focusing on the "grim, dark pile" (396) of Wildfell Hall, the harsh aspect of the unfamiliar landscape is redefined in the light of Helen's positive direction and hopeful vision of the future. Like the snowy wastes in *Agnes Grey*, Wildfell's "bleak and barren fields" represent the *tabula rasa* of Helen's future. Her new-found authority is articulated when she authors this change, defining her own inward beginning afresh, regardless of how outwardly bleak the prospect seems: "the bleak and barren fields beyond might have struck me as gloomy enough at another time, but now, each separate object seemed to echo back my own exhilarating sense of hope and freedom" (397). It would have been more obvious (and less like Anne Brontë) to show her heroine in a sunny, comfortable place, but making distinctions comparable to those made between Wuthering Heights and Thrushcross Grange in Emily's novel, Anne here distinguishes Helen's "desolate wilderness" from the softer, conservative surroundings like Linden Car where women know the limits of their place. Helen's "lonely spot" points to her existence as one of singular courage which is not cushioned from hard truth. Her decision to flee takes her into physical discomfort, but it also puts her in touch with the solid reality of moral rectitude and spiritual integrity.

The atmosphere of the hills and vales around Wildfell Hall provides a definite contrast to the repression that pervades the Park at Grass-dale. Wildfell Hall, true to its name, stands on land which is wild and open where Helen can wander at will. Thus free, she is often pictured rambling over the moorland in idyllic concert with her son, as Gilbert almost enviously remarks:

> But sometimes, I saw her myself,—not only when she came to church, but when she was out on the hills with her son, whether taking a long, purpose-like walk, or—on specially fine days—leisurely rambling over the moor or the bleak pasture-lands, surrounding the old Hall, herself with a book in her hand, her son gambolling about her. (47)

At Grass-dale, however, she had been virtually imprisoned within socially structured boundaries, such as those of her marriage. Thus pent up, she is vulnerable to further assaults on her liberty through the unwelcome advances of Walter Hargrave who would keep her imprisoned in dependent shame. In this stifling atmosphere of beleaguered virtue, the tension is mitigated somewhat by a warmly humorous picture of sisterly collaboration, when the faithful Rachel is shown acting as lookout against the possible incursion of a predatory Hargrave:

> descrying the enemy's movements from her elevation at the nursery window, she would give me a quiet intimation, if she saw me preparing for a walk. . . . I would then defer my ramble or confine myself for that day to the park and gardens. (334)

Although in this instance Rachel would appear to be colluding in Helen's confinement to the park (her intelligence helping to restrict her mistress's movements with good reason), her help is ultimately instrumental in freeing Helen from the marital prison. The significance of Rachel's role here goes beyond the time-honored figure of the faithful servant, for Helen's appreciation of this "sharp-sighted woman" (334) she calls her "friend" indicates Anne Brontë's acknowledgment of a potential community among women. Rachel's importance in the narrative makes a pragmatic argument for a supportive female presence as an essential part of Helen's survival and escape.

For the dénouement of the Grass-dale narrative, Anne Brontë uses two evocative symbols of entrapment to depict Helen's state. Her confusion and manipulation at the hands of both Huntingdon and Hargrave are symbolized in images of the maze and the chess game. When Helen cries out that she cannot bear to leave her child "in this dark and wicked world alone, without a friend to guide him through its weary mazes, to warn him of its thousand snares" (327), the biblical tonalities of "wicked" and "snares" reflect back on the abused mother who would protect her vulnerable child. Her entrapment is so destructive that she can say, "I am weary of this life," an expression of crushing disorientation that parallels the "weary mazes" she fears in her son's life (327). That she is outmaneuvered in the deadly game of sexual politics is explicit in Hargrave's triumphant shout of "Beaten—beaten!" when he wins the chess game, after Helen realizes that the snare of this "more serious contest" has even more ominous meanings: "A few more moves and I was inextricably entangled in the snare of my antagonist" (301). But her acute awareness of each cunning move along the way fits their dialogue with an ironical bite. When Hargrave asks Helen whether she acknowledges his superiority, without hesitation she astutely counters, "Yes—as a chess-player" (302), the irony of which is that she may well have lost the game but certainly not the more important struggle.

Immediately following this exchange, Brontë places the scene of Huntingdon's botched liaison with Annabella which draws attention even more pointedly to the discernible parallels between the gambits or maneuvers of the chess game and those carefully plotted moves that almost allow Huntingdon to dupe Helen sexually under her very nose. Hargrave's *double entendres*, with Hattersley's suppressed guffaws, and the mysterious comings and goings of Grimsby, Huntingdon and Annabella as they set up their assignation in the shrubbery behind Helen's back, would be faintly comical if it were not for the underlying seriousness of abuse. Seen in the light of Helen's innocent trust and genuine devotion, these deliberately misleading antics lend a muddled intensity to the scene that embodies Helen's psychological confusion. Lost in a maze of puzzling signs, Helen asks a series of anxious questions about the meaning of all this, and tries to make sense of Hargrave's innuendo about her husband and Annabella:

> Why did he laugh? Why did Hargrave connect them thus together? Was it true, then?—And was this the dreadful secret he had wished to reveal to me? I must know—and that quickly. (302)

After reading her opponent's motives so clearly in the chess game, Helen becomes vulnerable and loses her composure when she no longer knows the rules. Seen in the context of images such as the game's "combat" and "snare" in which she feels "inextricably entangled" (301), her confounded position exemplifies the abused woman who is trammelled in ignorance. Similarly, the ambiguous reference to "death among the trees" which Anne Brontë inserts with heavy irony into Helen's dialogue with Huntindgon demonstrates the confusing experience of betrayal and abuse. The disparity between the idiomatic meaning and the literal meaning of this doubly threatening "death" indicates the psychic destruction that lurks beneath the structures (or games) of social conformity.

> "It is a night that will give you your death, in another minute. Run away, do!"
> "Do you see my death among those trees, Arthur?" said I, for he was gazing intently at the shrubs, as if he saw it coming, and I was reluctant to leave him, in my new-found happiness and revival of hope and love. But he grew angry at my delay, so I kissed him and ran back to the house. (298)

Wrapped in this deliberate confusion, the true meaning behind the entity among the trees later emerges in the shape of his mistress. The death reference foreshadows the devastating impact of Helen's later discovery of infidelity, and the dialogue's ironic misinterpretations of language reveal two people hopelessly at variance with each other.

These images of death, entrapment, combat and disorientation (the maze) build the emotional atmosphere in preparation for the crucial discovery scene, where moon and nature imagery combine to evoke a liberating epiphany. Here, as in *Agnes Grey* (and Charlotte Brontë's *Jane Eyre*), moon imagery represents a strong *éclaircissement* and the empowering presence of divine grace, while the nature imagery in this passage becomes, as Ewbank puts it, "an integral part of an emotion and a spiritual state:"[30]

> "God help me now!" I murmured, sinking on my knees among the damp weeds and brushwood that surrounded me, and looking up at the moonlit sky, through the scant foliage above . . . until a gust of wind swept over me, which, while it scattered the dead leaves, like blighted hopes, around, cooled

my forehead, and seemed a little to revive my sinking frame. Then, while I lifted up my soul in speechless, earnest application, some heavenly influence seemed to strengthen me within: I breathed more freely; my vision cleared; I saw distinctly the pure moon shining on, and the light clouds skimming the clear, dark sky; and then, I saw the eternal stars twinkling down upon me; I knew their God was mine, and He was strong to save and swift to hear.

(304-305)

After this rapturous flood of positive reinforcement from a heavenly source, Anne Brontë goes on to make a pointed contrast between the spiritually empowering, emotionally comforting outdoors (connecting the onlooker to a limitless cosmos) and the suffocating constriction of social forms that contain Helen within structures of oppression.

Compared with the expansive clarity of the moonlit outdoors where she is set free in time and space, the artificial constraints that limit her within the confines of the house, surrounded by fixtures that suggest her own objectification, betoken imprisonment, disease and death:

Much of my newborn strength and courage forsook me, I confess, as I entered it, and shut out the fresh wind and the glorious sky: everything I saw and heard seemed to sicken my heart—the hall, the lamp, the staircase, the doors of the different apartments, the social sound of talk and laughter from the drawing-room. How could I bear my future life? In this house, among those people—Oh, how could I endure to live?   (305)

These juxtaposed images of enlightened liberation and stifling oppression make it clear that life, for Helen, must lie elsewhere, away from traditional material structures—the hall, the lamp, the staircase—through which is inscribed the disheartening patriarchal ownership of the entire establishment. The resounding message that emerges from the house itself changes all the former implications of her position as wife in the conservative social structure of marriage. Her only hope of survival is to find an alternative way of living; she must restructure a separate life to transcend the base hypocrisy and hierarchical impediments—"the social sounds"—that enforce an inner death.

To give Anne Brontë her egalitarian due, she does show that this problem is shared by both sexes; for Gilbert also faces the inhibiting walls of a stifling social structure as he journeys down the long, rough lane back to Linden-Car's softer regions from the "savage wilderness" of Wildfell Hall. The rough road to the Hall carries with it ironic messages about patriarchal tradition, which resides down in the vale, while autonomous freedom clearly stands in the opposite direction up at the Hall. Emphasizing the conflicting pull between Wildfell Hall and Linden-Car, the path image also suggests the contrasting promise of independent harmony which is given to Helen and Gilbert on the "hard, white, sunny road" to the sea (61). Winifred Gérin points out that for Anne Brontë the sea is often a "great liberator."[31] Certainly liberation is writ large in the picture of Helen and Gilbert, united "along the steep, stony hill" on a "loftier, more precipitous eminence" over the sea, despite the repressive warning from "some of the ladies" who "told her it was a frightful place, and advised her not to attempt it" (63). This vantage point on the seacliff offers a sign of their higher potential when unencumbered by social shibboleths and restraints.

If one compares Anne Brontë's treatment of sea and sky as images of freedom, it appears that the sea, although an agent of liberation, is also very much a reflection of individual potential. The liberating forces of the sea's tidal depths equate with the confident self-awareness prompted in Helen by this dynamic, "not deadly calm," but living water (62). The sea thus symbolizes both personal scope and powerful individual depths. The sea, with its restless waters, "covered with glinting breakers" (62), is implicitly connected to the soul of those who observe it. Anne Brontë juxtaposes this "deep violet blue" sea with Gilbert's comment on Helen's eyes, which are deeply colored like oceanic depths ("dark grey") and "full of soul" (62). Clearly, her communion with the sea from a "more precipitous eminence" says a good deal about the expansive inner dimensions of her consciousness (63). The sky, on the other hand, tends to reflect less of the individual state, and more of the "placid" constancy that speaks of God. Lord Lowborough's groaning "agony" at his wife Annabella's infidelity is witnessed by a "placid sky" (346), bringing to mind what Helen identifies as the "rapturous repose" of heaven. But, unlike Helen and Gilbert, he cannot discern such heavenly comfort because of his bitterness and lack of "that sustaining power of self-esteem," as he travels "blinded, deafened, bewildered," unable to repose "in Heaven's eternal sunshine" on the rough passage ahead (351).

Also difficult, but blessed by the love of a profoundly "good" woman, Gilbert's journey differs from Lowborough's in that his eyes and heart are opened to radical change; he experiences a kind of social and emotional enlightenment. In the early part of the novel before Helen's diary entries take over the narrative, Gilbert's love for this eccentric woman enables him to venture quite a distance from his repressively patriarchal beginnings. Yet, having journeyed from the embowered safety of his home to the airy heights of Helen's refuge and, even farther, to the heady sea-cliff "eminence," where he and Helen look out at the world in a brief moment of unison, Gilbert still has one last journey to make. Placed at the end of the narrative, this final journey will take him, as the isolated cliff-top foreshadows, to a place far beyond his original niche. The emotional difficulties of this last move are figured in the material impediment of a heavy snowfall, which (as for Agnes Grey) provides visual correlation for Gilbert's inner state of insecurity. His approach is literally and metaphorically snowed under with fears that the woman he loves has risen beyond his reach in the social structure to resume "her proper sphere" (483):

> But the night was long and dark; the snow heavily clogged the wheels and balled the horses' feet; the animals were consumedly lazy, the coachmen most execrably cautious, the passengers confoundedly apathetic in their supine indifference to the rate of our progression. (471)

Although, as this expressive catalogue of scornful analysis attests, Gilbert can overcome these physical obstacles in a commandingly masculine way, the social barrier of Helen's estate finally confounds him. The alienating effect which this situation has on the increasingly anxious Gilbert is pointed in an unexpected comic scene. Through the colorful conversation of two local characters who inflict upon him their own preconceived notions of rank and propriety (never far from property or possession in the scale of things), the disconcerted Gilbert is given pause to reflect on the whole business of hierarchical social forms:

> "There'll be lots to speak for her!—'fraid there's no chance for uz"—(facetiously jogging me with his elbow, as well as his companion)—"ha, ha, ha! No offence, sir, I hope?" (to me) "Ahem!—I should think she'll marry none but a nobleman, myself. Look ye, sir," resumed he, turning to his other neighbour, and pointing past me with his umbrella, "that's the Hall—grand park, you see—and all them woods—plenty of timber there, and lots of game—"
> (482)

In the mode of Shakespearean figures like the "hempen homespuns" of Bottom's company, these rough country characters express with brash mechanical precision the underlying truths about social difference. Even as it steps beyond the bounds of social nicety itself, the speech here conveys more about boundaries than map or treatise could, and Gilbert is rudely reminded that he does not fit the socially constructed pattern of material equality.

Gilbert's inward reaction to these socially imposed barriers to their love is extreme enough to prompt the question "Sickly Sir?" at the sight of his pallor (483), as he mistakenly ascribes his fears of rejection to Helen's "own sense of prudence and the fitness of things" (484). Again, the percipient irony is that unlike the family at Linden-Car which judges her singular character to be a dangerously unsuitable match, Helen sees beyond any such limited notions of fitness. Brontë focalizes the latter part of the narrative in Gilbert's wavering mind to demonstrate that it takes the initiative of a strong and clear-sighted woman to jolt a man so afflicted out of his alienated state of inverted pride. Helen claims her right to rearrange the status quo by deciding to woo Gilbert herself—a liberated gesture of courtship that reverses conventional expectations. In an action usually associated with male wooing, Helen offers her chosen partner a rose and her hand, with all their symbolic promise of loving constancy. The window, through which Helen reaches to pick the Christmas rose, is another instance of Brontë's favorite image of a fragile and permeable surface which separates the inner world from the outer universe. Focalized in the consciousness of a vulnerable man in this provocative instance, the impression of the window signifies a borderline between being fixed in the past and going forth into the future; the act of looking out through the window describes an imaginative process wherein space and time coalesce and reveal "all that is" with pellucid simplicity.

At a climactic point earlier in the narrative, when Gilbert has finished reading Helen's diary, the window through which he "gazed abstractedly on the lovely face of nature" reveals a clearer perspective of his situation: "this chaos of thoughts and passions cleared away, giving place to two distinct emotions," both of which are essential steps on the path towards liberation—joy in knowing that Helen is true after all and remorse for his mistrust of her (403). The window's promise of larger expanses outside offers the chance to progress beyond social limits, to overcome imposed emotional barriers, and find a broader reality. Helen seizes her chance, offered by the symbolic window, to do more than merely *look*; she seizes life with both hands and takes action:

> she turned away her glittering eye and crimson cheek, and threw up the window and looked out, whether to calm her own excited feelings or to relieve her embarrassment,—or only to pluck that beautiful half-blown Christmas rose that grew upon the little shrub without, just peeking from the snow, that had hitherto, no doubt, defended it from the frost, and was now melting away in the sun. Pluck it however, she did. (491)

Working against this dramatic *grande geste* seen in Helen's emotional movement as she "threw up the window," the reductive "or only" neatly emphasizes a definitive sincerity in Helen's actions, just as the repetition of the word "pluck" demonstrates her decisiveness. The poetic language in this passage conveys a welter of passionate feelings, underscored by the paradoxically fragile tenacity of the winter rose. When Helen reaches out through the window, reaching figuratively beyond her past and present into the future, she dramatizes an unequivocal statement of Brontë's belief in egalitarian action. This scene affirms the possibility of stepping out beyond the impress of a limiting stereotype, to break through the static icon of angelic submission and become wholly alive. With her "glistening eye and crimson cheek," Helen is a picture of vitality, and the hardy rose itself could not more vividly symbolize strength and beauty attained with age and experience, as Helen herself makes clear:

> "This rose is not so fragrant as a summer flower, but it has stood through hardships none of *them* could bear: the cold rain of winter has sufficed to nourish it, and its faint sun to warm it; the bleak winds have not blanched it, or broken its stem, and the keen frost has not blighted it. Look, Gilbert, it is still fresh and blooming as a flower can be, with the cold snow even now on its petals.—Will you have it?" (491-92)

The flower which blooms in the snow is a composite symbol of life, love and maturity. Helen implicitly refers to the subtle beauties of mature love when she compares the rose with the more "fragrant" attractions of the "summer flower," for this resilient blossom mirrors her spiritual self, still blooming despite the "snow" of extraordinary hardships, physical and emotional.

Gilbert's inability to grasp her bold offer of love causes Helen to withdraw so rapidly that we see the perilousness of a move that works against the social grain. When it seems that her courageous step into the future is blocked by Gilbert's lack of vision, his entrenched traditionalism and social insecurity, Helen's reaction is a deeply significant return to the fire:

> Misconstruing this hesitation into indifference—or reluctance even—to accept her gift, Helen suddenly snatched it from my hand, threw it out on to the snow, shut down the window with an emphasis, and withdrew to the fire.
> (492)

In the context of such daring role reversal, the image has a definite impact: the old divisions are re-instated, the window to the future is shut down with the emphasis of fear, and life, for a moment, resumes its frozen stereotypical state "out on the snow," where the warmth of acceptance is denied; only the limited fireside role remains with its enclosed, uncreative heat. The retreat to the fireplace represents the consequences of both social and personal rejection: each side loses, in a return to hierarchical assumptions of place that confine different people to a "proper sphere" (483).

Throughout *The Tenant* and *Agnes Grey*, Anne Brontë demonstrates a profound understanding of the pain associated with unrequited love. Helen's gesture of throwing out the rose and shutting the window effectively describes her shutting out the already familiar pain of rejection. The situation recalls Agnes's temporary loss of Weston and Helen's earlier humiliation when her love for Arthur Huntingdon is crushed and thrown away. In both novels, Brontë's imagery explores emotional atrophy or "petrifaction" (325), as it had in poems such as "Self-Communion," where she relates a touchingly personal experience of lost or "withered" love. In that poem, referring to an inner winter that freezes the heart ("Nay but 'tis hard to *feel* that chill / Come creeping o'er the shuddering heart"), she explores the familiar fire that fades "For want of fuel," and goes on to describe petrifaction:

> To see the soft soil turned to stone
> For lack of kindly showers,
> To see those yearnings of the breast,
> Pining to bless and to be blessed,
> Drop withered, frozen one by one,
> Till centred in itself alone,
>   It wastes its blighted powers.   (*Poems* 156)

This important poem shows fire, winter and stone images linked, as in the novels, to emphasize the experience of isolation and wasted potential. As Anne Brontë works through the emotional and religious crises of the poem, she ultimately reaches a determined feeling of hope. As shown earlier, the closing lines point to a positive resolution, imagined as progress on life's path: "'Press forward, then, without complaint; / Labour and love—and such shall be thy meed'" (*Poems* 160). This is essentially the positive construct that is shaped by the imagery in the novels. Neither Helen nor Agnes is left with the poet's once "blighted powers." Their energy is not "centred in itself alone," and, like the Christmas rose in *The Tenant*, their yearnings do not "drop withered, frozen one by one," but flourish hardily and heartily. In reclaiming the rose thrown onto the snow, the "emblem" of Helen's heart, Gilbert accepts the offer of loving unity and steps forward like Helen, beyond the bounds of sexual and social division. Anne Brontë's choice of images here gestures towards the balance and growth of an egalitarian natural order.

CONCLUSION

"Her outward seeming and her inward mind"

The figurative worlds through which Anne Brontë leads her reader contain less of the bizarre or fantastic than those of her sisters' novels and poems, but their landscapes are nonetheless fascinating. The often commonplace symbolic landmarks lead into areas where "outward seeming" reveals the unexpected undercurrents of "inward mind" (*The Tenant* 121). Repeatedly, Anne Brontë confronts her reader with the social incongruities and dualities that inform her placement of images, and every turn of the narrative signals an enquiry into the problematical nature of accepted social "unities," such as marriage and the family.

I believe that Anne Brontë is more than the simple moralist of the Brontë sisters, and that her achievement as a writer far exceeded Charlotte's suggestion that her writing was only "a painful penance and a severe duty" meant to exorcise the demons of Branwell's alcoholism and her own "undreamt-of experiences of human nature" at Thorp Green.[1] Nor can she fairly be accused of "naiveté and religiosity," as Phyllis Bentley claims,[2] when the deeply provocative fabric of her poems and novels speaks so powerfully and cogently of re-defining orthodoxy.

Not only in its structure does *The Tenant of Wildfell Hall* attest to Anne Brontë's increasing maturity as an artist, but its dominant image patterns also display a contentious disquietude which advances the novel creatively beyond the more contemplative equanimity retained in *Agnes Grey*. Like some of the poems, *The Tenant* is shot through with extensively worked images of strife and seemingly irreconcilable polarities. Its symbolism explores the dualities of love and hate, good and evil, salvation and damnation, freedom and oppression, tracing a vital flux as these oppositions diverge and coalesce throughout the narrative process. Whereas *Agnes Grey* chronicles a woman's development through her quiet determination to survive independently, the self-realization that comes to the protagonists of *The Tenant* is won only through violent schism and radical break with tradition.

Anne Brontë's strategy is to present these distinct experiences and demonstrate their interrelatedness within the developing consciousness of each major character by using key images to show the shifts of awareness, the conflicts and reconciliations which occur as her protagonists progress towards self-realization. Her poetically configured studies of domestic strife and social division consistently represent the fruitlessness of the old way through psychological embodiment of the "petrifaction" and "bondage" which mark a life of servitude. Her exploration of the spiritual pull between enclosed domestic limits and natural open spaces and implies the tensions between maintaining repressive social hierarchies and breaking away from traditional structures.

Throughout her work she pictures the interplay of dualities by means of an antithetical image system: thus, images of light and shade, summer and winter, rock and sand, fire and ice, act as working sketches of the potential balance which exists in the natural order (as her God intends it) but which has not yet been realized in society. Anne Brontë's analysis of this external balance implies a belief that balance within the social structure can be achieved only in an egalitarian symbiosis between man and woman, mistress and servant, landowner and tenant. The image patterns in *Agnes Grey* and *The Tenant* map out the kind of co-equal endeavor which would erase or re-write that "hateful bondage" depicted in the chapter so aptly named "Dual Solitude" (*The Tenant* 322)

The egalitarian "truth" she expressly sets out to "reveal" at the start of her novels is precisely what Anne Brontë garners into the experiential cornucopia of her writings. Her Preface to *The Tenant* (like the authorial comments in *Agnes Grey*) shows an awareness of the demands placed on both reader and writer when choosing to follow a direction other than "the most agreeable course for a writer of fiction to pursue" (xxxviii). Enacting her depiction of the pilgrim's adherence to a risky "narrow way" in poems such as "Self-Communion," Anne Brontë herself chose to follow a rigorously probing path, to "reveal the snares and pitfalls of life to the young and thoughtless traveller" (xxxviii); it is a path she unfailingly adhered to in all her writings.

While the poems set out the patterns of her thinking, the novels flesh them out more fully and articulate more sharply the radical implications of those lyric utterances. Having emphasized her polemical intent at the beginning of both novels, she then proceeds to encode in her imagery the searing inscription that "there is no peace" without searching for the truth (*The Tenant* xxxviii). Her own philosophical and poetical search for truth reveals ambiguities and divisions, torment and "petrifaction." Yet, at the same time, she offers an unhesitating hope for balance and wholeness through the independent action of striving for good.

Both Helen and Agnes are shown determinedly setting out alone at critical moments when their footsteps are "the first to press the firm, unbroken sands" ahead (*Agnes Grey* 197). Their movements through the "vale of life" take each one into a pleasant domesticity which, on the surface, does not suggest too radical a departure from the norm, but their progress is clarified as independent and resolute despite all odds. The ultimate thrust of these texts is toward the need for creative and independent action on the part of male and female figures alike.

The creative freedom of real independence is objectified in the imagery that runs through both novels and poems. With definitive poise, Anne Brontë's bold painterly vision ranges from the narrow focus of the hearth to broader scapes of heath and restless water. The well-balanced world of her structural images inscribes these wittily sensible texts with the provocative and solid belief that emotional equilibrium gives rise to limitless intellectual possibilities. Anne Brontë's use of imagery directs the philosophical perspective of her writings beyond static social or sexual dichotomies, towards integration and progress.

NOTES

NOTES TO CHAPTER ONE

1. Anne Brontë, "Home," in Edward Chitham, *The Poems of Anne Brontë: A New Text and Commentary* (London: Macmillan, 1979), 100. All further citations from the poems are from Chitham and are cited by page number in the text.
2. In an exemplary piece of scholarship on the poems, Chitham urges the study of "Self-Communion" in particular. His recommendation points to a critical approach that has only infrequently been applied to Anne Brontë's work: "What Anne says in this poem ought to be studied with microscopic interest if we have any intention of arriving at a balanced view of her" (3). Close study of her poetic and fictional writings shows her on an equal footing with her sisters, although clearly separate from them in her approach.
3. Chitham, 194.
4. Angus Mason MacKay in *The Brontës: Fact and Fiction* (1897; rpt. New York: AMS Press, 1973), 21.
5. In a letter from Charlotte Brontë to W. S. Williams, 13 September 1850, in *The Brontës: Their Lives, Friendships and Correspondence*, 2 vols., ed. T. J. Wise and A. J. Symington (Oxford: The Shakespeare Head Press, 1980), II:157; subsequent references to the letters are from this edition, cited hereafter as *Correspondence*.
6. 5 September 1850, *Correspondence*, I:156.
7. "Novels of the Season," *North American Review*, 141 (October 1848): 354-69; in *The Brontës: The Critical Heritage*, ed. Miriam Allott (London: Routledge & Kegan Paul, 1974), 247.
8. Unsigned review, *The Atlas*, 22 January 1848, 59, in *The Critical Heritage*, 232-33.
9. *Westminster Review*, 47 (January 1848): 581-85, in *The Critical Heritage*, 87.
10. An exception here is Naomi Jacobs who says that both Emily and Anne use complex narrative techniques in order to tell "their anti-patriarchal truths" through male narrators (205). "Gender and Layered Narrative in *Wuthering Heights* and *The Tenant of Wildfell Hall*," *The Journal of Narrative Technique*, 16 (1986), 204-19.
11. Langland's survey of Anne Brontë's critics is particularly helpful, ranging as it does from the early reviews and Mrs. Gaskell's *Life of Charlotte Brontë* in the nineteenth century to current feminist critics. She points out that despite a rekindled interest in women writers, critics such as Patricia Spacks, Elaine Showalter, Sandra Gilbert, Susan Gubar, Nina Auerbach and Elizabeth Hardwick make only passing refer-

ence to Anne Brontë or mention her not at all in their important feminist reappraisals of the period. See *Anne Brontë: The Other One* (London: Macmillan, 1989), 148-58.

[12] 4 January 1848, *Correspondence*, I:175.

[13] See Ada Harrison and Derek Stanford, *Anne Brontë: Her Life and Work* (London: Methuen, 1959), 241.

[14] Letters to W. S. Williams, 14 December 1847, and 31 July 1848, *Correspondence*, I:162, 241.

[15] 5 September 1850, *Correspondence*, I: 156.

[16] *The Critical Heritage*, 402-403.

[17] *Conversations in Ebury Street* (New York: Boni and Liveright, 1924), 260-61.

[18] Will T. Hale, *Anne Brontë: Her Life and Writings* (Bloomington: Indiana University Press, 1929), called *Agnes Grey* "the barest sort of story, without color and without humor" (30). Clearly, the comic subtleties in Anne Brontë's clever reproductions of what Moore calls Yorkshire "patter" are lost on the unfamiliar ear of this midwestern American, whose scholarly opinion on the dialogue in *Agnes Grey* is astoundingly dim: "Every one," he observes, "uses big words and sentences that are too stiffly articulated" (ibid.).

[19] Chitham makes the case that Weightman is the most likely subject of this series of "love" poems. He concludes: "The man about whom the poems are written has some constant characteristics: a sunny smile, a light heart, a voice (silenced at last), and he is buried in the old church. The reader will make up his or her mind as to who is the subject of this series: but did *two* young men whom Anne knew well enough to romanticize both die in late 1842? It seems to me that all the circumstantial evidence fits William Weightman and no one else." *A Life of Anne Brontë* (Oxford: Blackwell, 1991), 63.

[20] Letter from Charlotte to her friend Ellen Nussey, 20 January 1842, *Correspondence*, I:228.

[21] I have used *The Clarendon Edition of The Novels of The Brontës*, general ed. Ian Jack: *Agnes Grey*, ed. Hilda Marsden and Robert Inglesfield (Oxford: Clarendon, 1988), and *The Tenant of Wildfell Hall*, ed. Herbert Rosengarten (Oxford: Clarendon, 1992); citations are given in the text.

[22] See Langland, *Anne Brontë: The Other One*, 43 and Chitham, *A Life of Anne Brontë*, 173.

[23] Harrison and Stanford, *Anne Brontë: Her Life and Works*, 194.

[24] See Chitham's Introduction to *The Poems*, 36.

[25] Although Inga-Stina Ewbank links *Agnes Grey* with the morality play, her insights into Anne Brontë's fiction are—far from trivializing—exemplary in their thoughtful analysis. *Their Proper Sphere: A Study of the Brontë Sisters as Early Victorian Female Novelists* (Cambridge, Massachusetts: Harvard University Press, 1966), 64.

[26] Ewbank, 49.

NOTES TO CHAPTER TWO

1. Ed. Hilda Marsden and Robert Inglesfield (Oxford: The Clarendon Press, 1988), 3.

2. Although I would question Inga-Stina Ewbank's assertion that Anne Brontë is a "moralist first and a woman second," it is clear from the prefatory statements in both *Agnes Grey* (at the beginning of Chapter 1) and *The Tenant* (in the preface to the second edition) that her purpose was to make moral sense of social problems. In response to suggestions that *Wuthering Heights* does not have a sense of good and evil, Ewbank emphasizes that it is an exploration of the "human condition" and its characters are "in various ways, presented as moral beings." I believe that an equally strong case can be made for reading Anne Brontë's fiction as an exploration of the "human condition" which, no less than the work of her sister, requires an unbiased and thorough approach. See Ewbank, *Their Proper Sphere* (Cambridge, Massachusetts: Harvard University Press, 1966), 85, 96.

3. One thing the other governess novels share is an emphasis on social inferiority. The governesses in Harriet Martineau's *Deerbrook* (1839) and Mrs. Sherwood's *Caroline Mordaunt* (1835) are stereotypes of angelic self-sacrifice. See Ewbank's survey of the governess novels, *Their Proper Sphere*, 59-60.

4. The dove in the poem is, like Agnes, confined within a prison-like structure, and its view of the world beyond emphasizes the "despair" of its imprisonment:
   In vain! In vain! Thou canst not rise—
   Thy prison roof confines thee there;
   Its slender wires delude thine eyes,
   And quench thy longing with despair.
   "The Captive Dove," 31 October 1843, in Edward Chitham, ed., *The Poems of Anne Brontë* (London: Macmillan, 1979), 93.

5. See Edward Chitham and Tom Winnifrith, *Brontë Facts and Brontë Problems* (London: Macmillan, 1983), 99.

6. From a facsimile copied at The Brontë Parsonage Museum, Haworth. See also T. J. Wise and J. A. Symington, eds., *The Brontës: Their Lives, Friendships and Correspondence*, 2 vols. (Oxford: The Shakespeare Head Press, 1980), I:321.

7. I refer here to Julia Kristeva's idea that the radical linguistic force of the semiotic inside language redefines meanings through silence and contradiction. See, for example, "Stabat Mater," trans. Arthur Goldhammer, in *The Female Body in Western Culture*, ed. Susan Rubin Suleiman (Cambridge, Massachusetts: Harvard University Press, 1985), 109.

8. "'Imbecile Laughter' and 'Desperate Earnest' in *The Tenant of Wildfell Hall*," *Modern Language Quarterly*, 43 (1982): 354.

9. John Milton, *Paradise Lost*, in *Complete Poems and Major Prose*, ed. Merritt Y. Hughes (Indianapolis: Odyssey, 1981), IX:887, 1036.

10. Winifred Gérin, *Anne Brontë: A Biography* (London: Penguin, 1976), 145.

11. William Makepeace Thackeray, *The Four Georges*, ed. Hannaford Bennett (London: John Long, 1923), 149.

12. Tennyson, *In Memoriam*, in *Poems of Tennyson*, ed. Herbert Warren (Oxford: Oxford University Press, 1921), 349.
13. Unsigned review, *Christian Remembrancer*, 97 (July 1857): 87-105; in *The Brontës: The Critical Heritage*, ed. Miriam Allott (London: Routledge & Kegan Paul, 1974), 369.
14. In the Preface to the second edition of *The Tenant of Wildfell Hall*, ed. Herbert Rosengarten (Oxford: Clarendon, 1992), Anne Brontë asks her critics, "Is it better to reveal the snares and pitfalls of life to the young and thoughtless traveller, or to cover them with branches and flowers?" (xxxviii).
15. Virginia Woolf discusses both Charlotte and Emily Brontë in this essay on *Jane Eyre* and *Wuthering Heights*. *Collected Essays*, 4 vols. (London: The Hogarth Press, 1966), I:189.
16. *Flower Lore* (1879; rpt. Detroit: Singing Tree Press, 1972), 197, 201.
17. Jean Marsh indicates that many early nineteenth-century dictionaries of the language of flowers gave confusingly mixed meanings. But the confusion of entries in the dictionary part of Kate Greenaway's *The Illuminated Language of Flowers*, published in 1884, is sorted out by Marsh's cross-indexed entries in the modern reprint (London: Macdonald and Jane's Publishers, 1978), 17, 48, 56.
18. *Paradise Lost*, III:6. Milton's invocation of God's "holy Light" was clearly in Anne Brontë's mind as she wrote *Agnes Grey*, for she also refers (twice: 63, 208) to the dark and deep "world of waters" (III:11) invested by that Light; see Hilda Marsden's and Robert Inglesfield's notes to the Clarendon edition.
19. See Ian Watt, *The Rise of the Novel* (Berkeley: University of California Press, 1957), 337-40. On the woman as moralist, see also Janet Todd, *The Sign of Angellica: Women, Writing and Fiction, 1660-1800* (New York: Columbia University Press, 1989), 228.
20. Robert Barnard, "Anne Brontë: The Unknown Sister," *Edda* 78 (1978): 33-38.
21. For elements of parody in *The Tenant*, see Edward Chitham and Tom Winnifrith, *Brontë Facts and Brontë Problems* (London: Macmillan, 1983), 104.
22. P. J. M. Scott, "*Agnes Grey*: Accommodating Reality," chapter 1 in his study *Anne Brontë: A New Critical Assessment* (London: Vision Press, 1983), 31, 43.
23. Terry Eagleton, *Myths of Power: A Marxist Study of the Brontës* (London: Macmillan, 1975), 126.

NOTES TO CHAPTER THREE

1. Ed. Herbert Rosengarten (Oxford: Clarendon, 1992), xxxvii. Although "nonsence" appears thus in the *The Tenant*'s preface, the conventional spelling is used for the same phrase ("soft nonsense") in the final chapter of *Agnes Grey* (207).
2. However, as Winifred Gérin points out, *The Tenant* was enthusiastically received by the public when it was published, and, despite its present eclipse, "of all the Brontë novels, it had the greatest contemporary sale, with the one exception of *Jane Eyre*"; *Anne Brontë: A Biography* (London: Penguin, 1976), 260.

³ She continues, "The simple and natural—quiet description and simple pathos are, I think, Acton Bell's forte. I liked 'Agnes Grey' better than the present work"; *The Brontës: Their Lives, Friendships and Correspondence,* 2 vols., ed. T. J. Wise and J. A. Symington (Oxford: The Shakespeare Head Press, 1980), I:241.

⁴ Linking *The Tenant* with *Wuthering Heights,* she continues: "This structure, appropriated from the familiar gothic frame-tale, here serves several functions that are strongly gender-related: it exemplifies a process, necessary for both writer and reader, of passing through or going behind the official version of reality in order to approach a truth that the culture prefers to deny; it exemplifies the ways in which domestic reality is obscured by layers of conventional ideology; and it replicates a cultural split between male and female spheres that is shown to be at least one source of the tragedy at the center of the fictional world" (204). "Gender and Layered Narrative in *Wuthering Heights* and *The Tenant of Wildfell Hall,*" *The Journal of Narrative Technique,* 16 (Fall 1986): 204, 206.

⁵ George Moore, *Conversations in Ebury Street* (New York: Boni & Liveright, 1924), 253-54.

⁶ Sandra Gilbert and Susan Gubar pursue the question, "What does it mean to be a woman writer in a culture whose fundamental definitions of literary authority are . . . both overtly and covertly patriarchal?" They also make the following point, which seems to me a basis for understanding much of Anne Brontë's use of imagery in expressing her radical vision: "Not only do these precursors [exclusively male writers who symbolize authority and fail to define female consciousness] incarnate patriarchal authority (as our discussion of the metaphor of literary paternity argued), they attempt to enclose her in definitions of her person and her potential which, by reducing her to extreme stereotypes (angel, monster), drastically conflict with her own sense of self—that is, of her subjectivity, her autonomy, her creativity"; *The Madwoman in the Attic* (New Haven: Yale University Press, 1979), 45, 48.

⁷ *Anne Brontë: "The Tenant of Wildfell Hall": A Study and Reappraisal* (Leeds: Emeril, 1974), 10.

⁸ Terry Eagleton, *Myths of Power: A Marxist Study of the Brontës* (London: Macmillan, 1975), 136.

⁹ Phyllis Bentley, *The Brontës* (London: Arthur Barker, 1947), 109.

¹⁰ *Anne Brontë,* 61.

¹¹ Ewbank, *Their Proper Sphere* (Cambridge, Massachusetts: Harvard University Press, 1966), 75.

¹² *Myths of Power,* 123.

¹³ *Anne Brontë,* 41.

¹⁴ See *The Poems of Coventry Patmore* (London: Oxford University Press, 1949), ed. Frederick Page, 170-72 and 180-85. Patmore's poem deals with a particular "angel" image which was held dear at the time when Anne Brontë was writing. The sexual "love" he describes, however, is decidedly sadomasochistic in tone:
Of smiles and simple heaven grown tired,
He wickedly provokes her tears,
And when she weeps as he desired,

> Falls slain with ecstacies of fears;
> He blames her, though she has no fault,
> Except the folly to be his;
> He worships her, the more to exalt
> The profanation of a kiss.   (171)

15. "'Imbecile Laughter' and 'Desperate Earnest' in *The Tenant of Wildfell Hall*," *Modern Language Quarterly*, 43 (1982): 354.

16. *Their Proper Sphere*, 77.

17. *Paradise Lost*, in *Complete Poems and Major Prose*, ed. Merritt Y. Hughes (Indianapolis: Odyssey Press, 1957), IX:526, 531.

18. *Paradise Lost*, IX:708.

19. *Myths of Power*, 123.

20. *Their Proper Sphere*, 78.

21. Ewbank (77) links the poem with Huntingdon.

22. Bentley, *The Brontës*, 113-14. Bentley's assertion that Brontë heroines were peculiarly "northern women" is a moot point, but it is true that Helen displays the "stubborn, unbowed independence" that Bentley ascribes to "the heritage of northern English people"; more particularly, Helen has "that innate sense of equality with all the rest of the world" evinced by Agnes Grey when she announces, "for in *truth, I considered myself pretty nearly as good as the best of them*" (*Agnes Grey*, 111; emphasis added).

23. See also her notion of authorial equality in the Preface to the second edition: "All novels should be written for both men and women to read, and I am at a loss to conceive how a man should permit himself to write anything that would be really disgraceful to a woman, or why a woman should be censured for writing anything that would be proper and becoming for a man" (xxxix).

24. Patmore, *Poems*, 181.

25. Patmore, *Poems*, 185.

26. *Their Proper Sphere*, 68.

27. Unlike Anne Brontë's heroines, Patmore's conventional "angel" is noticeably deficient in her organs of articulation: "If none but her dear despot hears / She prattles like a child at play" (*Poems*, 180). A similarly disturbing picture emerges from the lines, "She loves him for his mastering air, / His power to do or guard from harm" (147).

28. Whereas similar comments have been made about Jane Austen's narrowness of focus without harming her literary reputation as a powerful writer, Bentley rather damagingly (and falsely) concludes that since Anne Brontë's vision was narrow, her mind was not "a genuinely powerful one" (*The Brontës*, 109).

29. Brontë's regard for Cowper appears in her tribute, "To Cowper" (1842): "The language of my inmost heart / I traced in every line" (*Poems*, 84).

30. *Their Proper Sphere*, 81.

31. *Anne Brontë*, 163.

NOTES TO THE CONCLUSION

1. Charlotte's views were expressed in a letter of 5 September 1850 to W. S. Williams; see T. J. Wise and J. A. Symington, eds., *The Brontës: Their Lives Friendships and Correspondence*, 2 vols. (Oxford: The Shakespeare Head Press, 1980), II:156. The latter phrase regarding "undreamt-of experiences" is Anne's own, in her birthday note of 1845; see Winifred Gérin, *Anne Brontë: A Biography* (London: Penguin, 1976), 209.
2. Phyllis Bentley, *The Brontës* (London: Arthur Barker, 1947), 109.

BIBLIOGRAPHY

PRIMARY SOURCES

Brontë, Anne. *Agnes Grey*. Ed. Hilda Marsden and Robert Inglesfield. Vol. IV of *The Clarendon Edition of the Novels of the Brontës*. 7 vols. Oxford: Oxford University Press, 1988.

———. *The Tenant of Wildfell Hall*. Ed. Herbert Rosengarten. Vol. VII of *The Clarendon Edition of the Novels of the Brontës*. 7 vols. Oxford: Oxford University Press, 1992.

———. *The Poems of Anne Brontë: A New Text and Commentary*. Ed. Edward Chitham. London: Macmillan, 1979.

Milton, John. *Paradise Lost*. In *John Milton: Complete Poems and Major Prose*. Ed. Merritt Y. Hughes. Indianapolis: Odyssey Press, 1957.

More, Hannah. *Works*. London, 1803. Vols. II and III.

Patmore, Coventry. *The Angel in the House*. In *The Poems of Coventry Patmore*. Ed. Frederick Page. London: Oxford University Press, 1949.

Tennyson, Alfred. *In Memoriam*. In *Poems of Tennyson*. Ed. Herbert Warren. London: Oxford University Press, 1921.

Thackeray, William Makepeace. *The Four Georges*. Ed. Hannaford Bennett. London: John Long, 1923.

Wollstonecraft, Mary. *The Wrongs of Woman*. In *Mary; and, The Wrongs of Woman*. Ed. Gary Kelly. Oxford: Oxford University Press, 1976.

SECONDARY SOURCES

Allott, Miriam, ed. *The Brontës: The Critical Heritage*. London: Routledge & Kegan Paul, 1974.

Barnard, Robert. "Anne Brontë: The Unknown Sister." *Edda* 78 (1978): 33-38.

Bell, A. Craig. *Anne Brontë: "The Tenant of Wildfell Hall": A Study and Reappraisal*. Leeds: Emeril Publications, 1974.

Bentley, Phyllis. *The Brontës*. London: Arthur Barker, 1947.

Briggs, Asa. *Victorian People : A Reassessment of Persons and Themes, 1851-67*. Chicago: The University of Chicago Press, 1972.

Carruthers, Miss. *Flower Lore: The Teachings of Flowers*. 1879. Reprint. Detroit: Singing Tree Press, 1972.

Chitham, Edward. *A Life of Anne Brontë*. Oxford: Blackwell, 1991.

———, and Tom Winnifrith. *Brontë Facts and Brontë Problems*. London: Macmillan, 1983.

Eagleton, Terry. *Myths of Power: A Marxist Study of the Brontës*. London: Macmillan, 1975.

Ewbank, Inga-Stina. *Their Proper Sphere: A Study of the Brontë Sisters as Early-Victorian Female Novelists*. Cambridge, Massachusetts: Harvard University Press, 1966.

Gérin, Winifred. *Anne Brontë: A Biography*. London: Penguin, 1976.

Gilbert, Sandra, and Susan Gubar. *The Madwoman in the Attic*. New Haven: Yale University Press, 1979.

Greenaway, Kate, and Jean Marsh. *The Illustrated Language of Flowers*. 1884. Reprint. London: Macdonald and Jane's, 1978.

Hale, Will T. *Anne Brontë: Her Life and Writings*. Bloomington: Indiana University Press, 1929.

Harrison, Ada, and Derek Stanford. *Anne Brontë: Her Life and Work*. London: Methuen, 1959.

Jacobs, Naomi A. "Gender and Layered Narrative in *Wuthering Heights* and *The Tenant of Wildfell Hall*." *The Journal of Narrative Technique* 16 (1986): 204-19.

Kristeva, Julia. "Stabat Mater." Trans. Arthur Goldhammer. In *The Female Body in Western Culture*. Ed. Susan Rubin Suleiman. Cambridge, Massachusetts: Harvard University Press, 1985.

Langland, Elizabeth. *Anne Brontë: The Other One*. London: Macmillan, 1989.

McKay, Angus Mason. *The Brontës: Fact and Fiction*. 1897. Reprint. New York: AMS Press, 1973.

McMaster, Juliet. "'Imbecile Laughter' and 'Desperate Earnest' in *The Tenant of Wildfell Hall*." *Modern Language Quarterly* 43 (1982): 352-68.

Moore, George. *Conversations in Ebury Street*. New York: Boni & Liveright, 1924.

Reid, T. Wemyss. *Charlotte Brontë: A Monograph*. London: Macmillan, 1877.

Scott, P. J. M. *Anne Brontë: A New Critical Assessment*. London: Vision Press, 1983.

Tiffany, Lewis K. "Charlotte and Anne's Literary Reputation." *Brontë Society Transactions* 16 (1974): 284-87.

Todd, Janet. *The Sign of Angellica: Women, Writing and Fiction, 1660-1800*. New York: Columbia University Press, 1989.

Watt, Ian. *The Rise of the Novel: Studies in Defoe, Richardson and Fielding*. Berkeley: University of California Press, 1957.

Woolf, Virginia. *Collected Essays*. Ed. Leonard Woolf. 4 vols. London: The Hogarth Press, 1966.

Wise, T. J., and J. A. Symington, eds. *The Brontës: Their Lives, Friendships and Correspondence*. 2 vols. Oxford: The Shakespeare Head Press, 1980.

ENGLISH LITERARY STUDIES MONOGRAPH SERIES

1975   1 *Samuel Johnson's Library: An Annotated Guide,* Donald Greene
        2 *The Sale Catalogue of Samuel Johnson's Library: A Facsimile Edition,* J. D. Fleeman
        3 *Swift's Vision of Evil: A Comparative Study of "A Tale of a Tub" and "Gulliver's Travels,"* Volume I, *A Tale of a Tub,* Philip Pinkus
        4 *Swift's Vision of Evil,* Volume II, *Gulliver's Travels,* Philip Pinkus

1976   5 *Dryden and Future Shock,* William Frost
        6 *Henry Fielding's "Tom Jones" and the Romance Tradition,* Henry K. Miller.
        7 *The Achievement of Thomas More,* Richard J. Schoeck

1977   8 *The Postromantic Consciousness of Ezra Pound,* George Bornstein
        9 *Eighteenth-Century Arguments for Immortality and Johnson's "Rasselas,"* R. G. Walker
      10 *E. M. Forster's Posthumous Fiction,* Norman Page

1978 11 *Paradise in the Age of Milton,* U. Milo Kaufmann
      12 *The Slandered Woman in Shakespeare,* Joyce H. Sexton
      13 *Jane Austen on Love,* Juliet McMaster
      14 *C. S. Lewis's "Great War" with Owen Barfield,* Lionel Adey

1979 15 *The Arnoldian Principle of Flexibility,* William Robbins
      16 *Frankenstein's Creation: The Book, The Monster, and Human Reality,* David Ketterer
      17 *Christopher Smart's Verse Translation of Horace's "Odes,"* Arthur Sherbo, ed.
      18 *Gertrude Stein: Autobiography and the Problem of Narration,* Shirley Neuman

1980 19 *Daniel Defoe's Moral and Rhetorical Ideas,* Robert James Merrett
      20 *Studies in Robertson Davies' Deptford Trilogy,* R. G. Lawrence and S. L. Macey, eds.
      21 *Pater and His Early Critics,* Franklin E. Court

1981 22 *The Curve of Return: D. H. Lawrence's Travel Books,* Del Ivan Janik
      23 *The Educational World of Daniel Defoe,* Donald P. Leinster-Mackay
      24 *The Libraries of George Eliot and George Henry Lewes,* William Baker

1982 25 *John Ruskin and Alfred Hunt: New Letters and the Record of a Friendship,* R. Secor
      26 *The Cover of the Mask: The Autobiographers in Charlotte Brontë's Fiction,* A. Tromley
      27 *Charles Olson and Edward Dahlberg: A Portrait of a Friendship,* John Cech

1983 28 *The Road From Horton: Looking Backwards in "Lycidas,"* J. Martin Evans
      29 *Dryden's Dualities,* Ruth Salvaggio
      30 *The Return of the Good Soldier: Ford Madox Ford and Violet Hunt's 1917 Diary,* Robert Secor and Marie Secor

1984 31 *The Splintering Frame: The Later Fiction of H. G. Wells,* William J. Scheick
      32 *The Dynamic Self: Browning's Poetry of Duration,* Samuel L. Chell
      33 *George Moore's Correspondence with the Mysterious Countess,* David B. Eakin and Robert Langenfeld, eds.

1985	34	*Mother and Daughter Relationships in the Manawaka Works of Margaret Laurence*, Helen M. Buss
	35	*"Descend from Heav'n Urania": Milton's "Paradise Lost" and Raphael's Cycle in the "Stanza della Segnatura,"* Mindele Anne Treip
1986	36	*Upon The Ways: The Structure of "The Canterbury Tales,"* William E. Rogers
	37	*"Theatres of Greatness": A Revisionary View of Ford's "Perkin Warbeck,"* Dale B. J. Randall
1987	38	*Defoe and the Defense of Commerce*, Thomas K. Meier
	39	*A Bibliography of Johnsonian Studies, 1970-1985*, D. Greene and J. A. Vance
	40	*Browning's "Sordello" and the Aesthetics of Difficulty*, David E. Latané, Jr.
1988	41	*Lemon, Dickens, and "Mr. Nightingale's Diary": A Victorian Farce*, Leona W. Fisher
	42	*Anthony Trollope's Notes on the Old Drama*, Elizabeth R. Epperly
	43	*Perspectives on O'Neill: New Essays*, Shyamal Bagchee, ed.
1989	44	*Pope Versus Dryden: A Controversy in Letters to "The Gentleman's Magazine," 1789-1791*, Gretchen M. Foster
	45	*Isaac Reed, Editorial Factotum*, Arthur Sherbo
	46	*Critical Contexts of Sidney's "Astrophil and Stella" and Spenser's "Amoretti,"* Janet H. MacArthur
1990	47	*The Dream of My Brother: An Essay on Johnson's Authority*, Fredric V. Bogel
	48	*Blake's "Thel" and "Oothoon,"* Brian Wilkie
	49	*Richard Aldington: Reappraisals*, Charles Doyle, ed.
	50	*Talking on Paper: Alexander Pope's Letters*, Wendy L. Jones
1991	51	*Chaucer and Gower: Difference, Mutuality, Exchange*, R. F. Yeager, ed.
	52	*Spenser's Poetics of Prophecy in "The Faerie Queene" V*, Kenneth Borris
	53	*The Clerical Character in George Eliot's Fiction*, Oliver Lovesey
1992	54	*Coleridge: Historian of Ideas*, Charles De Paolo
	55	*Critical Essays on John Henry Newman*, Ed Block, Jr., ed.
1993	56	*Incest Narratives and the Structure of Gower's "Confessio Amantis,"* G. Donavin
	57	*"Th' Interpretation of the Time": The Dramaturgy of Shakespeare's Roman Plays*, Krystyna Kujawinska-Courtney
	58	*Congreve's Comedies*, Arthur W. Hoffman
	59	*Frames in James: "The Tragic Muse," "The Turn of the Screw," "What Maisie Knew," and "The Ambassadors,"* Paul G. Beidler
	60	*Selected Essays on the Humor of Lawrence Durrell*, Betsy Nichols, Frank Kersnowski and James Nichols, eds.
1994	61	*Time, Literature and the Arts: Essays in Honor of Samuel L. Macey*, T. R. Cleary, ed.
	62	*Anne Brontë's Radical Vision: Structures of Consciousness*, Elizabeth Hollis Berry
	63	*His "Incalculable" Influence on Others: Essays on Robert Frost in Our Time*, Earl J. Wilcox, ed.